River Oaks Centre

A Keyboarding and Word Processing Simulation

5th Edition

Arvella Adair, Ed.D.
Retired Teacher, Commerce High School and
Texas A&M University
Commerce, Texas

Karen Young
Former Teacher, Newman Smith High School
Carrollton, Texas

SOUTH-WESTERN
CENGAGE Learning

Australia • Brazil • Japan • Korea • Mexico • Singapore • Spain • United Kingdom • United States

SOUTH-WESTERN
CENGAGE Learning

River Oaks Centre: A Keyboarding and Word Processing Simulation

Arvella Adair, Karen Young

Editor-in-Chief:
Jack Calhoun

Vice President/ Executive Publisher:
Dave Shaut

Team Leader:
Karen Schmohe

Acquisitions Editor:
Jane Congdon

Executive Marketing Manager:
Carol Volz

Marketing Manager:
Mike Cloran

Marketing Coordinator:
Cira Brown

Production Editors:
Kim Kusnerak, Alan Biondi

Consulting Editor:
Marianne Miller

Production Manager:
Tricia Matthews Boies

Manufacturing Coordinator:
Charlene Taylor

Compositor:
Cover to Cover Publishing, Inc.

Printer:
Webcom

Design Project Manager:
Stacy Jenkins Shirley

Cover/Internal Designer:
Pagliaro Graphic Design

Cover Photo:
© PhotoDisc, Inc.

Clip art on pages 96, 97, 99, and 103 courtesy of free-graphics.com.

Table of Contents

Preface

River Oaks Centre was written to provide an interesting and realistic approach for students to integrate keyboarding, formatting, and word processing skills into a real-life work experience. River Oaks helps students make the transition from classroom to job. This simulation is for intermediate keyboarding students; however, Challenge Activities are included for more advanced students. Some of the features of River Oaks Centre are listed below.

- The simulation is non-software-specific and can, therefore, be used with various software packages.
- The new tech-savvy version includes Internet usage, e-mail, and web sites to stimulate and maintain student interest.
- A Resource Guide included in the back of the simulation provides examples and formatting guidelines for each job.
- River Oaks provides sound instruction while providing a change for students from the traditional classroom setting.
- Since the simulation incorporates Challenge Activities and Internet Activities, it can be used to challenge many different skill levels.
- New Internet Activities provide opportunities for students to become more familiar with Internet concepts through jobs that combine research and critical-thinking skills.
- River Oaks provides solid learning through the preparation of a variety of documents requiring students to use formatting and word processing skills.
- This simulation provides students with the opportunity to work independently to give them the experience of a real-life business office.
- Jobs and activities provide students with the experience of keying material from rough draft, script, and printed copy.
- Instructions are embedded within each job to ensure that students can work with little or no assistance from the instructor.
- The simulation assists students in organizing, setting goals, following written instructions, and working independently.
- Many of the jobs and activities within the simulation present a cross-curricular theme.

About the Authors

Dr. Arvella Adair received her doctorate in education from the University of North Texas. She taught business subjects on secondary and university levels for over 30 years in Texas, Oklahoma, and Tennessee. She received a national award as Outstanding Business Teacher of the Year from the National Business Education Association. She has authored seven publications and numerous articles in professional publications.

Karen Young earned her bachelor's degree in marketing from the University of North Texas. She also attained a Business Composite teaching certification from North Texas. She was a teacher at Newman Smith High School in Carrollton, Texas, where she taught keyboarding, business law, and other business courses. She currently travels to various school districts throughout the state of Texas to train teachers on specialized educational software. She is a software trainer, author, wife, and mother of two precious children.

Welcome to River Oaks Centre

Congratulations! With the assistance of your school's job placement program, you have been employed to work part-time in the Management Office at River Oaks Centre. On this job, you will use the skills you have acquired in keyboarding, computer applications, and other business courses.

Elizabeth L. Clark, Marketing Director, will assign work to you. You will be responsible for keying business documents including letters, memorandums, forms, tables, and news releases. The documents you complete will represent River Oaks Centre as well as you and your school. You are expected to finish each job accurately and efficiently.

Your work at River Oaks Centre will be interesting and fulfilling. It will give you the opportunity to key documents with which you are already familiar, such as letters and memorandums. It will also allow you to work with new documents such as newsletters, legal documents, and others. You will be required to make some decisions as you work on the heavily edited copy. This simulation will help you better understand the everyday occurrences in an actual business setting. Remember, do your very best work and have fun!

INFORMATION ABOUT THE CENTRE

River Oaks Centre opened in September of 2001. The Centre has 6 anchor stores, 186 retail stores, and 28 restaurants. Connected to the Centre is the luxurious five-star River Oaks Hotel. The Centre and hotel are located in Dallas, Texas.

Listed below are the executives for River Oaks Centre.

Title	Executive
General Manager	*Christian T. Brock*
Marketing Director	*Elizabeth L. Clark*
Leasing Manager	*Hamilton Schrauff*
Operations Director	*Christy Schall*
Chief of Security	*Scott K. Williams*

Below are the street address, phone and fax numbers, and web site of River Oaks Centre.

2701 Rochelle Drive
Dallas, TX 75260-4244

Phone:	*(972) 555-0101*
Fax:	*(972) 555-0179*
Web site:	*www.riveroakscentre.com*

GENERAL INSTRUCTIONS

Read all instructions thoroughly before beginning a job. Pay special attention to instructions written on a job by your supervisor, Elizabeth L. Clark (elc). Be sure to complete each job in the order presented. Since this is your simulation, you may write in the book.

Bulleted instructions are provided at the bottom of each job. Because different word processing software uses different names for various features, generic terms for those features have been used. Check with your instructor for more specific information about what word processing features to use in the jobs.

A few of the jobs will instruct you to print your final work on stationery provided in the back of this book. Simply tear out the stationery and feed it into your printer. Depending on your printer, you may need to adjust your paper size before printing. Your instructor will review specific printing instructions with you. Make sure you have reviewed your work thoroughly before printing since only one sheet of stationery is provided for a job.

Proofread each completed job carefully and correct all errors. River Oaks Centre takes great pride in producing neat and accurate business documents that represent the Centre in a professional manner.

USING THE RESOURCE GUIDE

The Resource Guide on pages 71–96 contains information and examples of the types of jobs you will be completing. Example 1 of the Resource Guide lists common proofreaders' marks. You will want to become familiar with these since you will be using them often in your work.

You will be instructed to refer to specific examples in the Resource Guide as you work through the jobs. The information in this Guide will be very helpful and valuable to you. Since you have these examples as a reference, you will be expected to work independently without assistance from your instructor.

TURNING IN COMPLETED JOBS

After you have completed the first five jobs, place them in numeric order. Tear out the Evaluation Form, and place it on top of your completed jobs. Write your name, the date, and your comments on the Evaluation Form. Attach the Evaluation Form to your five completed jobs, and give your work to your instructor. You will repeat the same procedure when you complete Jobs 6–10, Jobs 11–15, Jobs 16–20, and Jobs 21–25.

A Progress Report is provided on page 4 for you to keep track of your completed work and grades. As you complete each job, record the date on your progress report. When you turn in a group of five jobs to your instructor, record the date on your Progress Report. After the documents are returned to you, record the date and your grade on the appropriate lines. This will assist you in keeping your work organized and tracking your accomplishments.

RETRIEVING AND SAVING DOCUMENTS

Your instructor will most likely download selected data files onto your school server for you to retrieve to complete selected jobs in the simulation. If your instructor uses a different forum to get these files to you, he or she will review that in detail with you. These files are the River Oaks Centre letterhead and logo and rough drafts of selected jobs you will need to prepare the final copy. Each of these selected jobs will include instructions for you to open a specific file.

Your instructor will give you detailed instructions on how to open the files you need. He or she will also inform you on how to name and save your completed work. Make sure you use the Save As feature to rename and save your completed jobs to ensure that you do not save your work over the original data file.

CHALLENGE ACTIVITIES AND INTERNET ACTIVITIES

Challenge Activities and Internet Activities are included in the back of this simulation. The Challenge Activities may be used at your instructor's discretion for additional work or as bonus activities. The Challenge Activities provide practice in more advanced formatting and word processing skills.

The Internet Activities will help you become more familiar with accessing web sites, connecting to links, and using search engines to find information. An Internet Activity icon is included with specific jobs. Your instructor will inform you if he or she wants you to incorporate the Internet Activities in with your regular work or complete the activities as a separate unit at the end of the simulation. These activities will require you to use both your creativity and critical-thinking skills.

Your supervisor, Elizabeth L. Clark, and your instructor are sure you will find your work at River Oaks Centre to be a rewarding experience and an excellent opportunity to improve your keyboarding, formatting, and word processing skills. Many of the jobs require you to make creative decisions. The activities in this simulation are similar to jobs you will complete when you are employed full-time. Enjoy your experience working at River Oaks Centre!

Fill in this form as you complete your work.

Job Completed	Date Completed	Date Jobs Turned In	Date Jobs Returned	Grade Received
Job 1	_____			
Job 2	_____			
Job 3	_____			
Job 4	_____			
Job 5	_____			
Jobs 1–5		_____	_____	_____
Job 6	_____			
Job 7	_____			
Job 8	_____			
Job 9	_____			
Job 10	_____			
Jobs 6–10		_____	_____	_____
Job 11	_____			
Job 12	_____			
Job 13	_____			
Job 14	_____			
Job 15	_____			
Jobs 11–15		_____	_____	_____
Job 16	_____			
Job 17	_____			
Job 18	_____			
Job 19	_____			
Job 20	_____			
Jobs 16–20		_____	_____	_____
Job 21	_____			
Job 22	_____			
Job 23	_____			
Job 24	_____			
Job 25	_____			
Jobs 21–25		_____	_____	_____

News Release
For Release: Upon Receipt
Contact: Elizabeth L. Clark

DALLAS, TX, August 28, 20—. Susan Jones can get to River Oaks Centre from her North Dallas home in five minutes. Last year it took her about 30 minutes to trek to the nearest Centre. Ms. Jones gladly makes this short commute to the new River Oaks Centre.

River Oaks Centre will celebrate its first year in business on Saturday. The developer and tenants both agree that the first year has been an exceptional one—with the promise of an exciting future. Statistics regarding the Centre show that:

*Sales average $425 per square foot. That is $62 per square foot more than last year's average at a comparable New York-based mall. It is also well above the average for all U.S. enclosed malls where sales last year averaged $341 per square foot.

*According to city officials, River Oaks is largely responsible for the 156 percent increase in sales tax receipts in the last year. So far this year, Dallas has collected $21,678,034 in sales taxes, more than in all of last year.

*The national restaurant chain Gregory's Steak House chose River Oaks to open its first Dallas-based restaurant in 14 years. The restaurant based its decision on the reported number of people estimated to move into this North Dallas area in the next 20 years. The founders of Gregory's expect the River Oaks location to surpass the company's $14 million per store annual sales average in its first year.

Subtitle: Hub for Business

River Oaks already is the hub for almost 4 million square feet of retail and restaurant space. It houses 6 anchor stores and 186 retail stores and 28 restaurants. Immediately north of the Centre is an open-air shopping center that includes Wholesale Books, Elite Shoe Warehouse, and Walco among its tenants; and much more construction is on the way. In all directions around River Oaks, signs are posted announcing the opening of additional national retailers.

(Job 1 continued on p. 6)

Just west of the Centre, Dallas Bullets and Texas Spurs owner David Landes has plans for a $26 million minor-league ballpark and a $21 million Spurs training facility. This deal will solidify the area and be a big plus for retailers. Landes said, "The market there is so huge. This area is as good as it gets in terms of overall development."

Subtitle: Little Vacancy

Gregory's will be the Centre's 186th tenant. With its opening, River Oaks will be 99.6 percent leased, led by the original six anchor stores. Several big-name tenants have arrived since the grand opening. Davis & Nogle Booksellers, The Pizza Kitchen, The Kids Barn, and The Bedroom Shoppe are a few of the retailers to open their doors in River Oaks.

"This Centre fits the market better than any Centre I've been associated with," said River Oaks Centre's general manager, Christian Brock, who has 15 years' experience in management. Mr. Brock states, "The store lineup and the merchandising mix meet the needs of the market."

River Oaks meets the needs of an array of shoppers. The Centre attracts shoppers from several neighboring counties. "It's very complete," Mr. Brock said. "It's got specialty stores, department stores, restaurants, and entertainment venues. It has what you want and need. So, go forth and shop!"

- **Refer to Example 2 in the Resource Guide.**
- **Set margins to correct positions, and set line spacing to double-space.**
- **Use bullets feature to replace the asterisks in the list with a special character.**
- **Use hanging indent feature for the bulleted list.**
- **Use underline feature for subtitles.**
- **Spell check final work.**

September 1, 20--
Mr. Brent Taylor
1536 Broken Bow Lane
Seattle, WA 98121-2154
Dear Brent

Please key this letter and prepare an envelope. elc

The management of River Oaks Centre is delighted to learn that you and your family will be moving to Dallas when you become manager of Champion Sports. You will find the Centre's staff and other store managers to be very cooperative and willing to assist you in any way.

Getting settled in a new city can be difficult, especially locating appropriate housing. Dallas has a great number of housing developments near River Oaks Centre. Also, several cities near the Centre are great commuters' towns with excellent schools.

I have contacted a relocation specialist on your behalf. She can assist you in making the transition a smooth one. Her name is Cindy Perez, and she can be reached at (972) 555-0199. You may also want to e-mail her at cindyp@inet.net. She can provide you with information about the metroplex area including housing, transportation, sights, sports, entertainment, dining, and so on. I think you will find Dallas to be an exciting and interesting city.

The management at River Oaks Centre is looking forward to your arrival. Let us know when you reach Dallas, and we will make arrangements to introduce you to our staff and other store managers.

Sincerely

Elizabeth L. Clark
Marketing Director
xx

- **Use File: Letterhead.**
- **Refer to Examples 3 and 4 in the Resource Guide.**
- **Set margins to correct positions.**
- **Use automatic hyphenation.**
- **Use auto text to insert closing lines.**
- **Use envelope feature, selecting envelope size 6 3/4.**
- **Spell check final work.**
- **Replace xx with your initials.**

TO: Cindy Perez   (Or instructor's e-mail address)

FROM: Elizabeth L. Clark   (Or your e-mail address)

DATE: September 5, 20--   (Inserted automatically on the e-mail screen)

SUBJECT: RELOCATION OF MR. TAYLOR

As we discussed on August 29, Mr. Taylor is planning on moving to Dallas on October 15, 20--. He would like your assistance in locating housing in the area around River Oaks Centre. Some of the communities we discussed were Carrollton, Plano, and Frisco. He is interested in a three-bedroom house that is approximately 2,700 square feet.

Also, please send Mr. Taylor information regarding transportation, sights, sports, entertainment, and dining. He has a son who is very interested in soccer. I think Mr. Taylor and his son would appreciate receiving some information pertaining to club soccer teams.

Mr. Taylor's e-mail address is btaylor@inet.net. Please contact him directly to see if he and his family would like additional information. Thank you for your assistance.

- **Use the e-mail feature within your program.**
- **Send a copy to Brent Taylor.**
- **Spell check final work.**

TO: Participating Teen Xtreme Stores

FROM: Elizabeth L. Clark, Marketing Director

DATE: September 10, 20—

SUBJECT: TEEN XTREME

As you know, the Teen Xtreme event is this Sunday, September 15, from 6:30–9 p.m. We know this event will be a great success. Here are some of the final details.

 # > <u>Store Closing</u>
The Centre is closing at 6 *p.m.* as usual on Sunday. Your store can either keep your gates open at that point, or you can shut your gates to prepare for the event and reopen at 6:30 p.m. The "goodie bags" are not being passed out until 6:30 p.m. when the event officially ~~begins.~~ *will kick off*

 # > <u>Have Fun</u>
Remember to have fun and be creative during this *exciting* event! This is one time that the Centre actually encourages you to "bend" the rules. Turn your music up, decorate your store, pull racks into the Centre…the ideas are endless. *; provide refreshments*

 # > <u>Results</u>
Attached is a short results survey for you to fill out during *or immediately after* the event. We appreciate the time that you ~~and your staff~~ will spend on this, as the information will be ~~added~~ *tabulated* to determine the success of teen xtreme. Please return the form by Monday, September 16 *; before 6 p.m.* We are anticipating an Xtreme success, and afterward we will begin making plans for next year's event.

If you have any questions, please be sure to call *or e-mail* the Centre's office. *Thanks!*

xx

(Job 4 continued on p. 10)

- **Use File: Job 04.**
- **Refer to Example 5 in the Resource Guide.**
- **Set margins to correct positions and spacing of body to single-space.**
- **Use underline feature for subtitles.**
- **Change font size where directed in memo.**
- **Spell check final work.**
- **Replace xx with your initials.**

] Teen Xtreme [center and change font size to 36 pt.
] Retail Promotional Survey [center, bold, and change font size to 18 pt.

Name of retail establishment _____

Your position ~~(circle one)~~: Manager   Assistant Manager   Sales Clerk   Other

How was your overall store traffic?   Fantastic   Very good   Good   Fair   Poor

How would you rate your sales performance?   Fantastic   Very Good   Good   fair   poor

Did your establishment offer ~~a~~ ^any^ premium item?   Yes   No
        If yes, what?   _____

Did your establishment offer any sales coupons?   Yes   No
        If yes, how many were redeemed?   _____

Would you want to duplicate this promotion next year?
        _____   Absolutely. This was great for business.
        _____   Yes. We had a good turnout.
        ~~_____   I don't see why not~~ [
        _____   Its under consideration.
        _____   I don't think so.
        _____   Definitely not.
(optional)
Name ^ _____

Store _____ [

] Thanks for your ^input^ ~~time~~ and ~~your~~ particiation! [center and change font size to 18 pt.

] Please promptly return this form to the management office [center and change font size to 18 pt.
by 6:00 p.m. Monday, September 16, 20--.

- **Use File: Job 04.**
- **Use bold feature.**
- **Change font size as directed.**
- **Use centering feature.**
- **Use cut feature.**
- **Spell check final work.**
- **Change margins to fit survey to one page.**
- **Print final document on the stationery on p. 97.**

] Specialty Stores in River Oaks Centre [Bold, center font size to 18 pt.

Bag 'n Luggage .... Suite 1120

Baseball Dreams .... Suite 1162

Brookfield .... Suite 2243

Cutlery Incorporated .... Suite 2150

Matthew and Mary .... Suite 1238

Franklin Corry .... Suite 1067

Kiko's Newsstand .... Suite 2101

The Sunglass Hut .... Suite 1237

Swim 'n Ski .... Suite 1214

Where's My Hat? .... Suite 2048

- **Use File: Job 05.**
- **Use the dot leader tab feature.**
- **Format attractively on the page.**

Tear out this form, and hand it in to your instructor along with Jobs 1–5.

Name _____

Date _____

Student's Comments to Instructor_____

_____

_____

_____

_____

The following is to be completed by your instructor.

		Points Possible	Points Achieved
Job 1	News Release	25	_____
Job 2	Personal Business Letter with Envelope	25	_____
Job 3	E-mail	10	_____
Job 4	Interoffice Memo and Survey	20	_____
Job 5	Business Form: Directory	20	_____
	TOTAL POINTS	100	_____

Instructor's Comments to Student_____

_____

_____

_____

_____

River Oaks Centre Management
Office will be closed
from 1:30-3:30 p.m.
on Monday, September 23,
for a staff training session.
If you need security,
call (972) 555-0101.
Thank you.

This announcement
should be in all
caps and boldface.
elc

(Job 6 continued on p. 16)

- **Use File: Job 06.**
- **Refer to Example 6 in the Resource Guide.**
- **Change line spacing to double.**
- **Use change case feature.**
- **Use center alignment for both vertical and horizontal spacing.**
- **Use bold feature.**
- **Insert a hard page break at end of announcement.**

River Oaks Centre Staff Training

Date	Time	Topic	Room
Sept. 23, 20--	1:30–3:30 p.m.	Web Pages	101
Sept. 30, 20--	1:30–3:30 p.m.	New Employees	100
Oct. 6, 20--	3:30–5:30 p.m.	E-mail	100
Oct. 14, 20--	3:30–5:30 p.m.	Centre Security	102
Oct. 21, 20--	6:30–8:30 p.m.	Publicity	101
Oct. 28, 20--	6:30–8:30 p.m.	Merchandising	100

Please key this table. The title should be in all caps and boldface. The column headings should be boldface. etc

- **Refer to Example 7 in the Resource Guide.**
- **Use automatic table feature for schedule.**

Elizabeth L. Clark

Professor Noland

Marketing Management

24 September, 20—

I prepared this paper for my course at TMU. I will also present this report to the general manager. Please prepare final copy in MLA format. etc

City of Dallas, Texas

Welcome to Dallas—a city that is so much Texas, and yet so much more! ~~It's~~ *Dallas is* a warm and

friendly place with all the down-home charm you expect. It's also a vibrant, progressive city full

of people eager to share their bounty with the world. As our Dallas mayor expressed:

Indeed, Dallas has much to share. Where else can you find both the Super Bowl

Champions and a world-class symphony? To see how far Dallas has come, gaze up at the

green glow of the 72-story National Bank Tower; then walk a couple of blocks west to

find the primitive cabin of Dallas founder John Neely Bryant that was built in 1841 on a bluff

overlooking the Trinity River ~~in 1841~~.

Sights & Attractions

Dallas ~~is~~ *stands* among the great cultural and entertainment centers of the world. Dallas's newest

attraction is Pioneer Plaza, where a bronze statue tributes the cowboys of the old days. In Old

City Park just south of downtown, you can see firsthand what life was like in Dallas at the turn of

the century.

~~When it comes to~~ *Renowned* museums and galleries, Dallas ~~is the place to be~~ *flourish in* The Dallas Museum

of Art, The Women's Museum, and the African American Museum provide intriguing glimpses of

art and culture from around the world. Native flowers, shrubbery, and greenery can be enjoyed

at the Dallas Arboretum and *at* White Rock Lake.

(Job 7 continued on p. 18)

Arts and Entertainment

Throughout the city, the curtain goes up nightly on performances at Pegasus Theater, Hip Pocket Theater, Addison Theater Center, and the Undermain Theater. During the ~~mussmer~~ summer months, Broadway hits come to Dallas's prestigious Dalla^Summer Musicals.

Country music fans,^ and opry as well as symphony and opera lovers can hear top-quality ~~mucis~~ music in Dallas The Arts District downtown is home ~~of~~ to the Dallas Symphony Orchestra, and is the heart of Dallas's cultural scene.

Sports and Recreation

Dallas ~~is a city that~~ loves to complete! From professional sports to collegiate athletics and amateur events, spectators and ~~sportsmen~~ athletes alike find Dallas a great place to play. Dallas is one of few cities in the United states with a franchise from each of the major professional sports leagues. ~~Dallas is ahome to~~ professional teams of basketball, football, baseball, hockey, and soccer. all thrive in Dallas

The Dallas area also has numerous lakes. Fishing, sailing, water skiing, and various other water sports are readily available.

Transportation

With ~~a~~ such a central location, Dallas is home to one of the world's largest and busiest airports. More than 50 million people arrive in the area each year through DFW International airport. Also located in Dallas is Love Field Airport where over 10 million people arrive each year. Many smaller airfields are also located in the metroplex area.

The citizens of Dallas can ~~also~~ use the public bus system, which provides transportation throughout the city. New to the city is the Dallas rail system, a monorail that provides high-speed transportation from the suburbs to the down town area. ~~Dallas also has~~ an enormous array of other transportation facilities ~~which~~ makes Dallas truly the crossroads of North America.

(Job 7 continued on p. 19)

Dining

If you enjoy international food, you'll find Mediterranean, Chinese, Indian, Italian, and Middle Eastern just to name a few. A bevy of continental dining offers food and service above the rest with ambiance rivaling the most famous restaurants in the world. Whatever your culinary taste, you will find it in Dallas!

Dallas offers a delightful culinary choice with more than 5,000 restaurants serving a veritable smorgasbord of food and service from inexpensive "fast food" to haute cuisine. The local favorite is tex-mex. These spicy recipes include enchiladas, fajitas, chalupas, and sopillas with honey for dessert.

Works Cited

Dallas Official Visitors Guide. Publication of The Dallas Convention and Visitors Bureau. 1999-2000 ed. Dallas, Texas.

The Texas Almanac. Published by the Texas State Department of Publishing. 2001-2002 ed. Austin, Texas.

- **Use File: Job 07**
- **Refer to Example 8 in the Resource Guide.**
- **Use centering feature for title.**
- **Use hanging indent feature for quotation.**
- **Cut and paste paragraphs to be moved.**
- **Place Works Cited on a separate page.**
- **Use page numbering (with text) feature.**

(Current Date)
Mr. Sanjay Patel
Patel Display Company
6834 El Dorado Parkway
Tulsa, OK 74131-5987
Dear Mr. Patel:

River Oaks Centre is now accepting bids for Christmas decorations. Your bid should include illustrations depicting your creative ideas and specifications for holiday decor. The complete package will include installation, takedown, and storage.

Santa Claus will arrive Saturday, November 18, 20--. Therefore, the Santa set and decor must be completely installed by Thursday, November 16, in order to give us a couple of days to "fluff" and troubleshoot if necessary. Takedown of the set must begin immediately following Christmas and be completed no later than Friday, January 5, 20--.

Your bid should include the following:

- Illustrations of complete Centre decorations
- Cost of installation and takedown
- Cost of storage of the decorations
- Additional equipment you may need

Please let us know if you have any questions or require additional information in order to complete the bidding process. Thank you for your interest in this project.

Sincerely,

Elizabeth L. Clark
Marketing Director

xx

c   Tony Carimi
    Katie Carter

- **Use File: Letterhead.**
- **Refer to Example 9 in the Resource Guide.**
- **Set margins to correct positions.**
- **Use date feature to insert date.**
- **Use number feature to replace the bullets in the list.**
- **Use auto text to insert closing lines.**
- **Use envelope feature, size 10, and insert a delivery point barcode.**

To: All Store Managers
From: Management Office
Date: September 25, 20—
Subject: JOB VACANCIES AND REQUEST FORMS

Enclosed is a copy of the job vacancies now available at River Oaks Centre. This information will be posted at each entry to the Centre as well as at the Customer Service Desk.

Also enclosed is a request form to be used by your store to list job vacancies at your establishment. Please note that these requests are updated every Wednesday; therefore, the information needs to be submitted to the Marketing Assistant by 1 p.m. each Tuesday.

We hope this service will facilitate your staffing needs. Please let us know how we may assist you further here at River Oaks Centre. Your success is important to us.

xx
Enclosures

(Job 9 continued on p. 22)

- **Refer to Example 5 in the Resource Guide.**

- **Use the find and replace feature to change *job vacancies* to *employment opportunities*.**

EMPLOYMENT OPPORTUNITIES

September 25, 20—

DATE	STORE	CONTACT	PHONE	POSITION	COMMENTS
Sept. 1	The Cookie Company	Juan Gonzales	(972) 555-0127	Sales Associate	Flexible Hours
Sept. 8	Lisa Cole, Inc.	Trish Lancer	(972) 555-0154	Sales Associate	Part-time
Sept. 15	Eddie Beyer	Todd McCain	(972) 555-0113	Shift Leader	Must be over 18
Sept. 16	Children's Toy Place	Ying Jiang	(972) 555-0180	Manager	Some Weekends
Sept. 22	Annona's	Anna Hatch	(972) 555-0142	Sales	Great Benefits
Sept. 24	Crafters Eyewear	Jenn Donning	(972) 555-0166	Sales Associate	Flexible Hours

(Job 9 continued on p. 23)

- **Refer to Example 10 in the Resource Guide.**
- **Use automatic table feature.**
- **Bold, center, and shade the main title.**
- **Center-align column titles.**
- **Center-align the third column.**
- **Adjust column widths to fit the information.**

Employment Opportunities Request Form
Store Name   _____
Phone Number   _____
Manager or Contact Name _____
Position Available   _____
Comments   _____
              _____

Employment opportunities are updated every Wednesday. Please submit this form by 1 p.m. Tuesday to be included in the updated version. Unless we are notified otherwise, an employment opportunity will remain on the list for only 30 days.

Return this form to the Marketing Assistant in the Management Office or to the Customer Service Desk; you also may fax the form to (972) 555-0179.

- **Use information to create form.**

- **Use bold, centering, and font features where necessary.**

Join River Oak's Premier Shopping Club / *center, bold, and change font size to 26 pt.*
It's Complimentary!

You'll redieve: *to*

Font size 16 pt.

A complimentary coupon book with discounts at over 40 stores and restaurants *50*
Complimentary Shopping bags
Complimentary seasonal gift wrapping
Complimentary phone calls *local*
Complimentary gifts with purchase opportunities
And much, much more!

the
Join the Shopping Club at trh Customer Service Desk! *center, font size 20*
(Located on the lower level near Annona's) *center, font size 16*

- **Use find and replace feature to change *Complimentary* to *Free*.**
- **Add bullets to indented list.**
- **Change font size where directed.**
- **Use centering and bold feature where directed.**
- **Center horizontally and vertically on the page.**
- **Print final document on the stationery on p. 99.**

Tear out this form, and hand it in to your instructor along with Jobs 6–10.

Name _____

Date _____

Student's Comments to Instructor_____

_____

_____

_____

_____

The following is to be completed by your instructor.

		Points Possible	Points Achieved
Job 6	Announcement and Table	20	_____
Job 7	MLA Report with Works Cited	25	_____
Job 8	Block Letter with Envelope	15	_____
Job 9	Interoffice Memo, Table, and Request Form	25	_____
Job 10	Business Form: Flyer	15	_____
	TOTAL POINTS	100	_____

Instructor's Comments to Student_____

_____

_____

_____

_____

AGE DISTRIBUTION
RIVER OAKS CENTRE TRADE AREA

Age Distribution (In Years)	River Oaks Trade Area	Average in U.S. Malls	River Oaks Percentage +/- of U.S. Average
0-13	23%	21%	+2%
14-20	10%	9%	+1%
21-34	30%	22%	+8%
35-54	28%	27%	+1%
55-64	5%	8%	-3%
65+	4%	13%	-9%

- **Refer to Example 7 in the Resource Guide.**
- **Use the table feature.**
- **Change row height of title to .5.**
- **Join cells of title. Join cells of each subtitle.**
- **Insert a column for percentage information.**
- **Shade the title cell.**
- **Set alignment of all cells to center.**
- **Center table vertically and horizontally on the page.**

TO: River Oaks Centre Staff
FROM: Anna Hatch
DATE: October 8, 20--
SUBJECT: MINUTES OF MEETING

Attached are the minutes from the Tuesday, October 6, staff meeting. Please mark your calendars for the next meeting scheduled for Tuesday, November 5, at 8:30 a.m. in the Management Office.

If you are unable to attend, please notify my office. Your participation is encouraged so you can stay informed and provide input into the Centre's decisions.

xx

Attachment

(Job 12 continued on p. 29)

- **Refer to Example 5 in the Resource Guide.**
- **Set margins to correct positions.**

SUMMARY MINUTES RIVER OAKS CENTRE MERCHANTS ASSOCIATION MEETING
October 6, 20—

The regular monthly meeting of the ROC Merchants Assocation was held on Tuesday, October 6, 20—, in the Vista Room of the Centre. President Todd McCann called the meeting to order at 2 p.m.

Committee Members in Attendance: Elizabeth L. Clark, Marketing Director of River Oaks Centre; Christy Schall, Operations Director; Juan Gonzales, Manager of The Cookie Company; Trish Lancer, Manager of LisaCole, Inc.; Todd McCann, Manager of Eddie Beyer; Ying Jiang, Manager of Children's Toy Place; Anna Hatch, Manager of Annona's; Jenn Donning, Manager of Crafters Eyewear; and Mark Vogel, Manager of Vogel's Video Rentals, and Zoie Anderson, Manager of Teen Time.

Recorder of Minutes: Anna Hatch

1. The minutes of the September 4, 20—, meeting were read and approved.

2. Treasurer, Trish Lancer, reviewed the September financial statement. She stated that the media commitments remained the same in this report. The ROC Merchants Assocation account has a balance of $42,589.15.

3. The traffic count was approximately 150,000 for the Gazelle Car Promotion. Merchant sales were up and press articles were abundant. Jenn Donning said that her traffic was up and that she had the best weekend since before the Labor Day weekend. Mark Vogel stated that the tour people were exceptionally polite and courteous to customers and that there were no complaints. Juan Gonzales reported that the computers on the lower level stayed crowded with interested users.

4. Elizabeth L. Clark, Marketing Director of River Oaks Centre, noted that the Kathy on Tour promotion would be very large and complicated. She said the logo of Kathy on Tour looked great and announced that the company wants shots of all the dolls on the ice for a national promotional picture. The company also wants to videotape the entire Centre, including storefronts, displays, display windows, and the ice arena.

5. A special meeting is scheduled of the ROC Merchants Association next Tuesday at 2:00 p.m. in the Vista Room concerning the Mall Money promotion. Jenn Donning noted that this is a year-long promotion geared to the young, affluent shopper. Collection Cans will be printed with the logo of each sponsor. This special meeting is scheduled to last one hour.

6. Radio Station KETZ Giveaway is being sponsored by KETZ and Z-Cars. Z-Cars valued at $180,000 are presently displayed in the Centre. KEYZ is also providing $6,500 worth of publicity at no charge to our Centre. The total amount of this promotion is over $185,000 at absolutely no charge to the Centre or its tenants.

(Job 12 continued on p. 30)

Minutes ^   (Insert date of minutes)

2
QS

7. The "Bear-able" Magic Show will be an even bigger promotion than Kathy on Tour. Zack Black, son of Dick Black, and the national vice presidents of Corona Cola will be on hand. The local television station KEMM will videotape the show in its entirety.

8. Todd McCann, president, introduced Anita Sanchez of Sanchez Advertising. She has coordinated the entire Kathy on Tour promotion. She explained how this promotion is guaranteed to boost traffic and sales in the Centre. Anita Sanchez stated that she has been promised 6 o'clock news coverage.

9. President McCann declared that a special meeting would be called for Tuesday, October 13, at 2:00 in the Vista Room.
   ^p.m.

10. Mr. Jiang moved and Ms. Lancer seconded the action that the meeting be adjourned. The motion carried, and President McCann declared the meeting adjourned at 5 p.m.

- **Refer to Example 11 in the Resource Guide.**
- **Use numbering feature.**
- **Use find and replace feature to change *McCann* to *McCain*.**
- **Use automatic hyphenation feature.**
- **Preview your work before printing.**

First-QUARTER REPORT

The following *information* outlines the major activities accomplished at River Oaks Centre for the second quarter of this year.

Advertising

Continuation of the "Good values" Campaign was used to advertise the Sidewalk Sale and other promotional events. Advertising was delivered through direct mail, newspaper advertisements, and through radio spots on radio station KIKM. Value Club newspaper advertising appeared in *The Dallas News*, *The Richardson Evening News*, and *The Plano Star*.

Income Producing events

Two income-producing events were held during the second quarter, generating $18,359 in additional revenues to the Merchants Association. Handmade in America Show, and the May Sports Card show was coordinated through Huff's Promotions produced the April craft show. (Lott, 2000, 3)

Community Events

Four community events were held during the second quarter, drawing additional traffic flow and publicity to the Centre. The annual Space Coast Philharmonic Musicthon was held April 29 and 30. More than 75 students from Brevard's School of Music performed for shoppers throughout the weekend. The annual Dallas County Science Fair was held May 17 and 18 throughout the Centre. More than 200 science projects were displayed from students throughout the county. (Patterson Management Reports, 2000, 6-7)

(Job 13 continued on p. 32)

Letters of appreciation were received from several community leaders thanking River Oaks

Centre for supporting our schools and young people. Ms. McKenna Lorson, ~~our~~ *Dallas* city manager,

expressed her gratitude as follows:

(Job 13 continued on p. 33)

References

Lott, Chris.
River Oaks Monthly. Publication of river Oaks Centre, Summer 2000 ed.: 3.

Patterson, Shannon. Summit Mall Management Reports. Publication of Summit Mall Corporation, Spring/Summer 2000 ed.: 6-7.

- **Open File: Job 13.**
- **Make corrections and format according to Example 12 in the Resource Guide.**
- **Use indent feature for quotation.**
- **Use page numbering feature in the header.**
- **Use widow/orphan feature.**
- **Open File: Jones Letter. Cut the first paragraph from the letter, and paste it into this document as a quote in the last paragraph.**

TO: Centre Staff, Public Safety, and Housekeeping

FROM: Elizabeth L. Clar, Marketing Director

DATE: October 17, 20—

SUBJECT: Weekend Events

This Saturday for new stores in the Centre will be hosting their grand-opening activities. Please make the employees of these new storse feel welcome an assist them in making their opening day a big success.

The Washington Mint (lower level near Byte Site)

The Washington mint will have the faux pearls worn by Jackie Kennedy on display in the store on Friday and Saturday. A grand-opening ceremony will take place at noon. Hamilton Schrauff will be attending the event as a representative from Centre Management. Public Safety employees should be on hand to assist with crowd control.

Noah's New Ark (lower level near Annona's)

Noah's new Ark will host a variety of entertainment at its store on Saturday in honor of its grand opening. From 2 to 4 p.M., Millicent McCollock, author of *Story of Animals* will be on hand to autograph her book. Noah's New Ark has been given permission to set up a small autograph tabyle just outside their store. The store will also feature clowns, a balloon twister, and costume characters. Please note that they have been advised not to wander through the Centre or stop shoppers. The event will stay contained just in front of the store with the exception of the autograph table, which will be in place from 2 to 4 p.m.

Public Safety employees should be on hand to help with crowd control. If there is a need for barricades, please available be to help set them up. Make sure the clowns, costume characters, and balloon twister do not wander the Centre.

Champion Sports (lower level near Tansy's)

Champion Sports will conduct demonstrations of their Swiss-engineered "Kangaroo Jump," which is used in athletic training and aerobic exercises. Special carpet will be temporarily placed outside the store for the demonstratoins. Public Safety employees should monitor the demonstrations to ensure spectators do not get to close.

(Job 14 continued on p. 35)

Create-A-Bear (located on lower level near ice arena)

Create-A-Bear offers shoppers the chance to make life more "bearable" for children. Shoppers can turn unstuffed teddy bears into finished bears they creat_e with love. Bearamy, the store mascot will be outside the entrance to greet children. Public Safety employees should be aware that many children will be attending this opening event. Please be available at all times to keep a close watch on the children.

At the end of the day, each department should ~~call~~ *contact* my office and report on successes and problems created by the opening of these new stores in our Centre.

xx

- Refer to Example 5 in the Resource Guide.
- Find 23 errors in the document, and write in proofreaders' marks.
- Tear out pages and review with instructor.
- Open File: Job 14 and key changes to document.

RIVER OAKS CENTRE
IN-MALL SIGNAGE OPPORTUNITIES

River Oaks Centre offers promotional opportunities to its retailers to help promote sales and specials and generate store traffic. On a first-come basis, retailers can sign up to have their promotions advertised in the Centre on 22" × 28" posters and/or table tents in the food court. There is no promotional fee to participate. The following are guidelines for program involvement:

In-Mall Posters
Standard size is 22 inches × 28 inches.
Posters should advertise some type of sale and/or special for your store.
Posters must have two or more colors.
Maximum of eight posters to be displayed back-to-back in four of the five following areas:
Lower level ice arena
Lower level main entrance
Upper level Annona's court
Upper level Customer Service Desk
Upper level Tansy's court

Food Court Table Tents
Standard size is 4 inches × 6 inches.
Tents must have two or more colors.
Base of tent should be sturdy enough to accommodate entire tent.
Maximum of 250 tents.
Tents need to be assembled by your store and brought to the Centre's management office at least 24 hours before scheduled placement in the food court.

If you wish to participate, please fill out the appropriate form available from the Centre's office and submit it two weeks prior to the date you are requesting tents and posters be displayed. All tents and posters must be preapproved by bringing a sample copy to the Centre's office. Please do not have tents or posters printed prior to approval.

Tents and posters will be displayed approximately seven days, and a store is able to participate in each program once per quarter. If you have questions, please contact the marketing department in the Centre's office at (972) 555-0199.

(Job 15 continued on p. 37)

- **Change font size of title to 18 pt. bold.**
- **Insert bold and underline features to subtitles.**
- **Insert bullets and hanging indents.**
- **Insert WordArt of "Shopping" to run along right side.**
- **Insert appropriate clip art in lower right corner.**
- **Print final document on the stationery on p. 101.**

Request for Table Tents or In-Mall Posters

Today's Date _____
Store Name _____
Store Manager _____
Store Phone Number _____
Number of Table Tents _____
Number of In-Mall Posters _____
Request Begin Date _____
Request End Date _____

Please do not write below the following line (for Management approval only).
_____

Date Submitted for Approval _____
Approved (YES or NO) _____
Comments _____
_____
_____
_____
Dates to Be Displayed_____
Marketing Director's Signature _____

- **Change font size of title to 18 pt. bold and underline.**
- **Change spacing of request form to double-space.**
- **Center-align information vertically and horizontally on page.**
- **Use line feature for line in center of page.**

Tear out this form, and hand it in to your instructor along with Jobs 11–15.

Name _____

Date _____

Student's Comments to Instructor_____

_____

_____

_____

_____

_____

The following is to be completed by your instructor.

		Points Possible	Points Achieved
Job 11	Four-Column Table with Headings	20	_____
Job 12	Interoffice Memo and Minutes	20	_____
Job 13	Unbound Report with Textual Citations and References	20	_____
Job 14	Interoffice Memo	20	_____
Job 15	Business Form: Flyer and Request Form	20	_____
	TOTAL POINTS	100	_____

Instructor's Comments to Student_____

_____

_____

_____

_____

CALENDAR OF EVENTS

Job Fair—November 2: Collin County Community College and the Chamber of Commerce will host an area job fair. The fair will be held for two days at the college campus. No fee is required for your store to participate. The job fair will be promoted through various means including newspaper and radio (KDMX-103.9FM). Space is limited, so we need to know soon if you are interested in participating. The job fair is just one way for your store to find employees; we encourage you to research others.

Holiday Entertainment—November 26: Local choral groups are invited to sing and perform in the Centre just north of center court.

Olympic Week Theme—November 12: River Oaks Centre has been built on the strength of our desire to offer the finest shopping experience in North Dallas. We can think of no better way to celebrate our success than by throwing our collective spirit into supporting the Dallas 2012 bid to secure the Olympic games. With this in mind, River Oaks Centre has partnered with Dallas 2012 on the Preview Gala; and as evidenced by the events, we will take on a sports theme for the month. We encourage your store to participate by decorating your display windows with an Olympic/sports theme. The Gala will be tied in to the colors of gold, silver, and bronze and, of course, red, white, and blue.

Enter-to-Win—November 16: As part of the Christmas celebration, shoppers will be invited to register to win a variety of prizes including a new Santana PT Cruiser! Your store can participate in this program by donating a high-value prize. Your logo would then be featured in the Centre's advertising and signage concerning this program. Please call us to discuss the possibilities.

Behind the Scenes with *Soap Opera Review*—November 7: This event will give shoppers the opportunity to see what goes into designing the set of a soap opera, including the full regalia of equipment, and even perform in short scenes on stage with one of daytime TV's leading stars! Shoppers can also meet soap stars, get their autographs, and have photos taken with them.

2nd Annual River Fun Run—November 22: This 5K race, which benefits the Dallas Education Foundation, was held for the first time last year on the Centre's premises. River Oaks Centre provides beverages and snacks for participating runners and walkers.

Teen Event—November 28: This event by popular magazine *Teen Scoop* will provide teens with exciting interactive elements including live music, a fashion show, a casting call, a beauty station, and the latest trends. There will also be a karaoke machine and giveaways.

(Job 16 continued on p. 42)

River Oaks Centre Giving Tree—November 30: Starting on this date, local nonprofit agencies will display a "giving tree," where shoppers can pick up a tag with information about a child and his or her Christmas wishes. Shoppers can purchase those items and bring them back to the giving tree to drop off.

- Refer to Example 13 in the Resource Guide.
- Center, bold, underline, and change font size of title to 20 pt.
- Align document to justified.
- Use numbering feature.
- Use underline feature for event name.
- Use cut and paste to make document changes.
- Insert the page number in the upper right corner of second page.

(Current Date)

Miss Rosangela Dos Santos
Rosangela's
Rua Vicente Felix 342
01401-001 Sao Paulo
Brazil

Dear Miss Dos Santos:

RIVER OAKS CENTRE EVENTS

Your company has made a name for itself with your high-quality technology and artistic products. We are delighted you will bring your expertise to River Oaks Centre.

We have some events on the calendar in which your company may want to participate. If you need help in staffing your store before your opening, you might want to have someone from your company participate in our job fair. Also, we will be having an Olympic Week Event that will bring in lots of customers. The two events are detailed in the paragraphs below.

Sincerely,

Christy Schall
Operations Director

zy

Open your completed Job 16 file. Copy the first paragraph in Job 16 entitled Job Fair into this document as the third paragraph (do not include number, title, or date). Copy the third paragraph in Job 16 entitled Olympic Week Theme as the fourth paragraph of this document (do not include number, title, or date).

cs

- **Refer to Examples 4 and 14 in the Resource Guide.**
- **Open File: Letterhead.**
- **Set alignment of body to justified.**
- **Use envelope feature, selecting envelope size 10.**
- **Spell check your work.**

News Release

For Release: Upon Receipt

Contact: Elizabeth L. Clark

DALLAS, TX, October 18, 20—. River Oaks Centre, Dallas's newest upscale shopping venu is welcoming two new additions to the Centre. Opening will the The Ice and The Cheesecake Club next month. A THL regulation-sized rink will be the newest full-size, full-service rink in a shopping mall surpassing the reign of smaller mall rinks and hockey-only facilities. River Oaks Centre's ice arena will be available for skating and hockey classes, practices and games, and for shoppers and children looking to cool off in a cool way. River Oaks Centre plans to employ an experienced skating school director and a staff of figure skating coaches and instructors. It will feature learn-to skate classes, youth hockey clinics, group lessons and freestyle dance. Lessons.

"North Texas is making a name for itself in the skating world," said Rico Hernandez of Rink Management Corporation, a California-based company that will handle the facility's care operations "Skating and hockey are among the fastest-growing sports in America, and we're building the premier skating palace. We will combine the convenience of a shopping with a full-size, professionally managed competitive skating and hockey facility."

"The rink will be available for the Mike Modanos and Tara Lipinskis of Dallas as well as those who can't stand up on skates. Ice skating appeals to people of all ages and skill levels," said Joseph Dergston, first vice president of development for General Properties.

Also opening in the River Oaks Centre will be The Cheesecake Club, which began as a mom-and-pop establishment and turned into a Wall Street success story. The first Cheesecake Club opened in 1999 in Texas in Houston near the SouthPark Center at Southwest Highway and U.S. 45. It was an instant success.

The Cheesecake Club offers more than 200 menu items from mashed potato omelettes (mashed potatoes, smoked bacon, green onion, and sour cream) to barbeque chicken pizza (roasted chicken, smoked gouda, red onion, and cilantro). There's also the "Tons of Fun" Burger (2 beef patties, double cheese, a triple-decker sesame bun, onions, tomatoes, pickles, lettuce, and secret sauce). The menu lists more than 40 desserts including more than 30 different types of cheesecake (Key lime, white chocolate raspberry, and chocolate peanut butter cookie dough)

"If you're in the mood for an avocado roll, a classic burger, and a slice of choclate peanut butter cheesecake, The Cheesecake Club is the place to go," said Belinda Howard, Senior Development Director, General Properties. "It is an outstanding family restaurant and another great reason for families to visit River Oaks Centre."

(Job 18 continued on p. 45)

The Cheesecake Club will be right at home in the new 1.6 million-square-foot Centre. The restaurants distinctive architecture, stylish decor, superior service, and innovative menu of more than 200 items will combing to create an overall dining experience with unparalleled value. River Oaks Centre is located on the north side of SH 121 between Preston Road and the Dallas North Tollway. The 130 acre site is located in what is called the "Golden Corridor" of the city of Dallas. The area is seeing a boom in new high-end housing developments that River Oaks Centre will serve.

###

- Refer to Example 2 in the Resource Guide.
- Set margins to correct positions.
- Set line spacing to double-space.

TO: Christian T. Brock   (Or instructor's e-mail address)

FROM: Christy Schall   (Or your e-mail address)

DATE: October 20, 20—   (Inserted automatically on the e-mail screen)

SUBJECT: CALENDAR OF EVENTS

We have organized the promotional events through next month. Several promotions are new, and we are extremely excited about them. Our biggest event, Olympic Week Theme, will greatly increase traffic flow in the Centre and should increase sales in all stores. We expect this one event to draw as many as 1,500 additional shoppers to the Centre.

Also, our 2nd Annual River Fun Run is scheduled for November 22. This was a huge success last year, and we are hopeful about the outcome of this year's event. With the addition of our Mall Walkers Club, we predict this event will have a 10 percent increase in participants over last year.

I have sent an attachment of the Calendar of Events along with this e-mail. Let me know if you have any questions regarding the calendar. We look forward to the outcome of all the events. We know each one will add to the success of River Oaks Centre.

- **Use the e-mail feature within your program.**
- **Attach your completed Job 16.**

- **Send a blind copy to Elizabeth L. Clark.**
- **Spell check your final work.**

- Make a notice for River Oaks Centre's bulletin board informing the tenants of the upcoming events.
- Gather the needed information to complete this form from the completed Calendar of Events (Job 16). Write the name and date of

the events on this form, tear it out, and ask your instructor to check it for accuracy.
- After you have received your instructor's approval, use the form to key an attractive announcement for the bulletin board.

Event

_____

_____

_____

_____

_____

_____

_____

Date

_____

_____

_____

_____

_____

_____

_____

- Open your completed File: Job 16.
- Use an interesting font, perhaps in color.
- Use WordArt.
- Print final document on the stationery on p. 103.

Tear out this form, and hand it in to your instructor along with Jobs 16–20.

Name _____

Date _____

Student's Comments to Instructor_____

_____

_____

_____

_____

The following is to be completed by your instructor.

		Points Possible	Points Achieved
Job 16	Business Form: Calendar of Events	25	_____
Job 17	Modified Block Letter with Envelope	20	_____
Job 18	News Release	25	_____
Job 19	E-mail with Attachment	15	_____
Job 20	Business Form: Notice for Bulletin Board	15	_____
	TOTAL POINTS	100	_____

Instructor's Comments to Student_____

_____

_____

_____

_____

(Current Date)

Miss Tracie Lum
Business Management Class
~~Cooper~~ Memorial High School
PO Box 1251
Cooper, TX 75432-0070

Dear Miss Lum

FUNTIME CAROUSEL

The project your class is working on sounds very interesting. In answer to your question regarding the profitability and marketing strategy of the carrousel in River Oaks Centre, I would first like to tell you something about our carrousel.

We have in our Centre a Funtime Carrousel that has been, for more than a century, the classic carrousel for Americans to ride. ~~They~~ are fun to ride and fun to watch. Our Centre is happy to be a part of a popular American tradition with a classic turn-of-the-century Tentsel-style carrousel from Funtime Rides.

Funtime Carrousels are true American classics with exquisitely detailed, handcrafted Wadley and Daye figures that trace their history back to the early 1900s. We chose this carrousel for our Centre because it has over 60 different horses and menagerie figures that create a delightful custom designed carrousel for the enjoyment of young and old alike.

The carrousel in our ~~Center~~ Byte Site Food court has proved to be a profitable marketing decision for our Centre ~~based upon~~ for the following ~~statements~~ reasons:

1. The carrousel puts the Centre in the forefront of today's retail marketing.

2. The innovative and creative use of the carrousel in a food court or common ~~space~~ area makes the Centre a destination for the entire family.

3. The carrousel increases the amount of time customers spend in the Centre.

4. The carrousel gives us an advantage in leasing space to retailers and distinguishes our Centre from the competition.

5. Nostalgic Americana sights and sounds create an exciting environment—the kind today's shoppers ~~want~~ desire.

(Job 21 continued on p. 52)

Our Funtime Carrousel provides a birthday party package. This package includes admission to ride the carrousel, a T-shirt for the birthday person, paper party products, and use of a private party room for 1 hour. Their own cakes, and drinks, and gifts may be brought into the private party room.

Good luck to you in completing your research for the class project. If you need any further information, please come by our Centre offices. We hope you find River Oaks Centre a fun place to shop and eat!

Sincerely

Elizabeth L. Clark
Marketing Director
xx

- Refer to Examples 4 and 15 in the Resource Guide.
- Open File: Letterhead.
- Key the letter address in USPS style.
- Use open punctuation.
- Use the find and replace feature to change *carrousel* to *carousel*.
- Use the numbering and hanging indent features for the list.
- Insert second-page heading.
- Use envelope feature, selecting envelope size 10.

TO: All Store Managers
FROM: Christy Schall, Operations Director
DATE: October 21, 20--
SUBJECT: TENANT INFORMATION SHEET

The Centre's office is compiling information on all our tenants. Most of the information will be kept confidential in our management offices. We will publish a directory that will include the following information for each store:

- Name
- Telephone number
- Suite number
- E-mail address
- Fax number
- Manager's name
- Assistant Manager's name

Once we receive all the information sheets, we will create a store directory. We will then provide one copy of the directory to each store.

Please complete the enclosed information sheet and return it to the Centre's office at your earliest convenience.

xx

Please key this memo and information sheet.
cs

(Job 22 continued on p. 54)

- **Refer to Example 5 in the Resource Guide.**
- **Use the bullet feature.**

- **Set margins on memo to correct positions.**
- **Insert page break at end of memo.**

TENANT INFORMATION SHEET

Store Name: _____

Suite Number: _____ E-mail Address: _____

Telephone Number: _____ Fax Number: _____

Store Manager: _____ Asst. Manager: _____

Corporate Office:

Address: _____

Phone: _____ Fax: _____ E-mail: _____

District Manager:

Name: _____

Address: _____

Phone: _____ Fax: _____ E-mail: _____

Store Insurance:

Company Name: _____

Address: _____

Phone: _____ Fax: _____ E-mail: _____

Mail Rental Invoices To:

Name: _____ Position: _____

Address: _____

Phone: _____ Fax: _____ E-mail: _____

Contact For Promotions/Advertising:

Name: _____

Address: _____

Phone: _____ Fax: _____ E-mail: _____

RETURN TO CHRISTY SCHALL IN THE CENTRES OFFICE AS SOON AS POSSIBLE.

- **Change margins on information sheet to fit on one page.**
- **Use your View/Print Preview feature frequently to check the appearance of your information sheet before printing.**

TO: Christian J. Brock   **(Or instructor's e-mail address)**

FROM: Elizabeth L. Clark   **(Or your e-mail address)**

DATE: October 25, 20--   **(Inserted automatically on the e-mail screen)**

SUBJECT: SEMINAR FOR STORE MANAGERS

A very important seminar will be held on November 15 from 8 a.m. to 5:30 p.m. in the Vista Room. Managers and assistant managers are invited to attend. Topics for discussion will include how to make the Centre more attractive, how to entice new tenants, how to renovate successfully, and how to improve the Centre's overall image within the Dallas community.

Coffee and assorted pastries will be available in the foyer of the Vista Room beginning at 7:45 a.m. Lunch will be provided at noon. Please come prepared to do some creative thinking and planning.

Attached is a copy of the agenda for the meeting. Please call the Centre's office and give us the names of those who will be representing your business.

Please send this e-mail with the agenda attached.
elc

(Job 23 continued on p. 56)

- **Use the e-mail feature within your program.**
- **Attach the following agenda.**
- **Spell check your final work.**

Agenda
River Oaks Centre
Seminar for Store Managers
November 15, 20--

8 a.m. to 9 a.m.--Registration and Refreshments

9 a.m.--"Mall Promotions--Some That Work and Some That Don't" by Marvin Washington, co-owner of Prestonwood Mall, Chicago, Illinois

10:30 a.m.--"Using Closed Hours Effectively" by Ben Dault, Public Relations Director, Ruth Jamison Associates, Shreveport, Louisiana

Noon to 1:30 p.m.-- LUNCH PROVIDED (in Jacques Room)

1:30 p.m.--"Renovation Plans" by Roberta Vazquez, owner, SCI Engineering

2:30 p.m.--"Operations Problems" by Christy Schall, Operations Director, River Oaks Centre

3:30 p.m.--"Marketing Update" by Francine Salvoni, Marketing Director, General Property Management

4:30 p.m.--"Update on Future Plans for Centre" by Christian J. Brock, General Manager, River Oaks Centre

All events will be conducted in the Vista Room.

- **Refer to Example 16 in the Resource Guide.**
- **Open File: Job 23 and make format changes.**
- **Send this as an attachment with the e-mail.**

October 28, 20—
Ms. Jacinta M. Guerra
Perfect Promotions
1924 Malone Drive
Tyler, TX 75703-1640

Dear Ms. Guerra:

[handwritten insert: Christmas Arts & Crafts Show]

Enclosed please find a copy of the agreement for the upcoming Christmas Arts & Crafts Show [handwritten: *is*] [handwritten: *promotional*] scheduled for December 10–16, 20—. Please sign [handwritten: *execute*] this agreement and return it to my attention [handwritten insert at left: *at River Oaks Centre*] along with the promotional and security fees. [handwritten: *and the security deposit*]

[handwritten: *In addition,*] I will send you a layout of the Centre indicating where the electrical and outlets are located and a map outlining the locations of the kiosks throughout the Centre. During the final walkthrough, we will relocate the kiosks as necessary.

Ms. Guerra, during your visit, I would like to sit down with you and finalize our Christmas Arts & Crafts Show plans. I look forward to working with you on another great craft show.

Sincerely,

Elizabeth L. Clark
Marketing Director

xx

Enclosure: Agreement

c Scott K. Williams

[handwritten note: Please key this letter and legal agreement. Make corrections as marked. elc]

(Job 24 continued on p. 58)

- **Refer to Examples 14 and 17 in the Resource Guide.**
- **Use the numbering feature for the list in the legal agreement.**
- **Use the page numbering feature to insert a page number on the second page of the legal agreement.**
- **Insert page breaks as needed.**

RIVER OAKS CENTRE

PROMOTIONAL AND ADVERTISING SE*R*VICE AGREEMENT

THIS promotional and advertising service agreement ("Agreement") made this _____ day of December, 20—, by and between RIVER OAKS CENTRE Merchants Association, Inc., a Texas Corporation ("Association"), and Perfect Promotions ("Promoter");

WITNESSETH:

WHEREAS, Promoter has agreed to perform certain promotional services which services may include, *but not limited to,* obtaining exhibitors ("Exhibitors") for activities at the River Oaks Centre ("Centre"), Dallas, Texas; and

WHEREAS, the Association is desirous of securing said services on the terms and conditions hereinbelow provided; and

~~WHEREAS, Promoter accepts such terms and conditions and agrees to be bound thereby;~~

NOW, THEREFORE, in consideration of the mutual convenants herein contained and other good and valuable consideration passing between the parties hereto, receipt and sufficiency of which is hereby acknowledged, be it agreed and committed as follows:

1. <u>Term.</u> That, the term of this Agreement shall commence on December 10, 20—, *unless sooner terminated as provided for herein.* and end on December 16, 20—.

2. <u>Promotional Event.</u> That Promoter shall provide and perform the following services ("Promotional Event"): One ~~Indoor~~ *Arts &* Craft Show, December 10–16, *20*—.

3. <u>Compensation of Association.</u> Promoter shall pay Association the sum of $6,000. The compensation shall be payable no later than twenty (20) days before the Promotional Event.

4. <u>Right of Review.</u> That Association may, at its sole discretion, *and at any time during the term of this Agreement,* eliminate any display which the Association determines is not in keeping with the character of the Centre.

(Job 24 continued on p. 59)

5. <u>Promoter's Insurance</u>. That Promoter shall maintain, *at its sole cost and expense,* insuranmce policies for workers' compensation and public liability.

IN WITNESS WHEREOF, the paarties hereto have hereunto set their hands and seals to this Agreement the day and year first above written at Dallas County, Texas:

Signed, Sealed and Delivered   RIVER OAKS CENTRE MERCHANTS
in the Presence of   ASSOCIATION, INC.

      (Corporate Seal)

_____   _____
("Promoter")   ("Association")

Inside The Centre

The Holiday Season Is Here!

According to research data from the National Board of Shopping Malls, approximately 27 percent of an average mall's total annual sales occur during the months of November and December. Furthermore, River Oaks Centre is estimated to welcome 3 million visitors during the months of November and December.

The holiday merchant meeting was held October 24. Stores received their Holiday Handbooks full of River Oaks Centre's holiday plans, hours, and safety tips. Please call the Centre's office if you have any questions.

Santa's Arrival!

Ho! Ho! Ho! Santa is on his way to River Oaks Centre.

On November 18, Santa will arrive for the season, making his grand entrance on a Dallas fire engine! Santa will be brought to the lower level of Annona's entrance, where awaiting children will greet him.

KGMI radio will conduct a live broadcast of its morning show beginning at 8 a.m. to promote Santa's arrival. The first 500 children at the event will receive a River Oaks Centre goodie bag with coupons from participating stores. Santa will arrive at 9:30 a.m. Children will be invited to escort him to his set, where he will read "The Night Before Christmas."

Doorbuster Bags!

To entice customers to shop River Oaks Centre the day after Thanksgiving, the Centre will reward the first 2,000 shoppers through the doors at 8 a.m. These 2,000 shoppers will receive a holiday bag full of goodies and coupons from participating stores!

This giveaway is being promoted through newspaper advertisements in *The Dallas News* as well as a variety of community papers and in-mall signage.

New Web Page Feature!

A new feature is available on the Centre's web page. It is called the Shopper Plus Club. This club is River Oaks shoppers' relationship marketing program.

When shoppers visit the Shopper Plus Club on our web page, they can register to become a member by submitting their personal information (name, address, e-mail, birthday, anniversary, and so on). They also indicate their shopping interests and expectations.

From now until December 31, 20—, there will be an extra incentive for the shoppers to become a Shopper Plus Club member. When a customer registers at www.riveroakscentre.com, he or she is able to choose ten offers or coupons from over 40 stores in the Centre. The coupons will be mailed to the customer's home within 14 days of receiving the on-line registration.

(Job 25 continued on p. 61)

- **Refer to Example 18 in the Resource Guide.**
- **Open File: Job 25.**
- **Format text into three newspaper-style columns.**
- **Turn hyphenation feature on.**
- **Set alignment of body to justified. Set alignment of titles to center.**
- **Use clip art and WordArt to produce a creative newsletter.**

(Instructions continued on next page.)

Welcome to Our New Stores!

<u>Wheels Galore!</u>
(Lower Level Annona's Wing)

<u>Cellular Cell</u>
(Upper Level Center Court)

<u>Fresh Market Bakery</u>
(Byte Site Food Court)

Kids Bake Off!

On Saturday, December 4, at 1 p.m., children will be invited to bring a treat they baked for Santa. Santa Claus and his elves will judge the contest, and prizes will be awarded to the top three treats.

The event will be promoted through newspaper advertisements and radio promotions on KRZP Kid Radio. Kid Radio will have a live remote at the event from 1 to 3 p.m.

Mall Management

Christian T. Brock, General Manager

Elizabeth L. Clark, Marketing Director

Hamilton Schrauff, Leasing Manager

Christy Schall, Operations Director

Scott K. Williams, Chief of Security

- **Change margins as needed to fit your creativity. Finished newsletter should be two pages.**
- **Use color, fonts, borders, and shading for creativity.**

- **Print your finished product on the paper provided in back of text (pp. 105 and 106).**

Tear out this form, and hand it in to your instructor along with Jobs 21–25.

Name _____

Date _____

Student's Comments to Instructor_____

_____

_____

_____

_____

The following is to be completed by your instructor.

		Points Possible	Points Achieved
Job 21	Two-Page Block Letter with Envelope	15	_____
Job 22	Interoffice Memo and Information Sheet	20	_____
Job 23	Interoffice Memo and Agenda	15	_____
Job 24	Modified Letter with Legal Agreement	20	_____
Job 25	Three-Column Newsletter	30	_____
	TOTAL POINTS	100	_____

Instructor's Comments to Student_____

_____

_____

_____

_____

Evaluation form 5

CHALLENGE ACTIVITIES

ACTIVITY ONE:
Return to your completed Job 7, which is an MLA report. This report was prepared for my Marketing Management class at the university but will also be sent to River Oaks Centre's General Manager, Christian T. Brock. Please compose a cover letter to accompany the report to Mr. Brock, explaining how the information in the report is useful to the Centre. Also, in the letter, inform Mr. Brock that I will be glad to meet with him to share additional information. Use the file: Letterhead.

ACTIVITY TWO:
Retrieve your completed Job 6. In the table, add these additional training courses:

Date	Time	Topic	Room
Nov. 6, 20—	6:30-8:30 p.m.	Internet	102
Nov. 14, 20—	3:30-5:30 p.m.	Promotions	101

Also, add the following information as the fifth column:

Speaker

Salmon

Cox

Salmon

Smith

Gomez

Cox

Davis

Chi

When completed, your new table should have ten rows (two for titles and eight for information) and five columns. You may need to adjust the column widths to make the table fit on one page.

ACTIVITY THREE:
Open your completed Job 13. Produce an outline from the unbound report. Use the outline feature of your word processing software.

ACTIVITY FOUR: Retrieve your completed Job 8. This letter needs to be mailed to three other display companies. Use the mail merge feature to supply the appropriate name, company name, and address for each letter. Make sure you change the name in the salutation. Open file: Letterhead. Print each letter on letterhead.

Mrs. Kari Diaz
Diaz Displays
1465 Preston Road
Dallas, TX 75248

Mr. Neil Milam
Milam Designs
9898 Castle Hills Drive
Carrollton, TX 75007

Mr. Bryan Chu
Promotional Display Company
5879 Menton Place
Frisco, TX 75034

ACTIVITY FIVE: Create a brochure promoting River Oaks Centre. Obtain the needed information from your completed Job 1. Use the brochure feature of your software to produce it. Be creative!

INTERNET ACTIVITIES

ACTIVITY ONE:

Plan a trip to Chicago to visit a competing mall. Locate the lowest price for airfare, car rental, and hotel. Use a search engine to find the following information:

- Airline carrier, flight number, and round-trip cost

- Rental car company name and cost per day

- Hotel name, address, and cost per night

- Driving directions from airport (O'Hare) to your hotel

Create, format, and print out an itinerary with all the necessary information. Submit it to your instructor.

ACTIVITY TWO:

Go to www.school.discovery.com. Select **For Students**. Click on **Presidential Library** to find and print a list of U.S. Presidents. Use that list to answer these questions:

1. How many Georges served as President between George Washington and George W. Bush?

   _____

2. Which two Presidents served only one year?

   _____

3. Which three men were President at some point during the year 1841?

   _____

4. Which President is your favorite and why?

   _____

Key the answers to these questions, and submit them to your instructor along with the printout of the list of Presidents.

ACTIVITY THREE:

Go to one of the web sites listed below to find an article related to **shopping and/or retail spending**. Conduct a search within the web site to find an article. Use the print screen feature to copy the text from the web site into a blank document in your word processing software. Print out the document, and submit it to your instructor.

www.usatoday.com

www.newsweek.com

www.nytimes.com

www.time.com

ACTIVITY FOUR:

Go to the **Occupational Outlook Handbook** on-line at www.bls.gov/oco/home.htm. Do a specific search on an occupation that interests you. Print the page from the web site that contains this information. Compose a paragraph describing why you are interested in this occupation. Turn in the printout from the web site and your keyed paragraph to your instructor.

ACTIVITY FIVE: Go to www.guinnessrecords.com. If you cannot open this web site, use one of these search engines: www.google.com, www.yahoo.com, or www.northernlight.com. Conduct a search to find the world's **largest shopping center**. Fill in the information below:

1. What is the name of the mall?
    _____

2. How many stores and services does the mall house?
    _____

3. How many department stores does the mall house?
    _____

4. What is the square footage of the mall?
    _____

5. Where is the mall located?
    _____

6. How much, in U.S. dollars, did it cost to build?
    _____

7. When was the mall built?
    _____

Print the page containing this information from the web site. Compile this information into a memo. Print out your memo, and turn it and the web site printout in to your instructor.

ACTIVITY SIX: Go to www.encyclopedia.com or www.bartleby.com/subjects. Do a search of **computer history** to find when computers originated. Key a short e-mail on what you find, and send it to your instructor.

ACTIVITY SEVEN: Go to www.disneyworld.com. Search the **Special Events** section to find an upcoming event. In an upcoming promotion, River Oaks Centre will be giving away a vacation trip for four to this event. Create a flyer promoting this event and the free giveaway of the trip. In the flyer, include details about the event, such as the event name, a brief synopsis of the event, dates, location, and so on. This flyer will be distributed to patrons of the Centre. Be creative!

ACTIVITY EIGHT: Go to www.nationalgeographic.org. Conduct a search to find a map of Europe. Answer the following questions:

1. What country is directly north of Austria?

   _____

2. What sea borders Denmark?

   _____

3. Which country is larger: Switzerland or Belgium?

   _____

4. What island is due west of the United Kingdom?

   _____

5. Which European country would you most like to visit and why?

   _____

Key the answers to these questions, and submit them to your instructor along with the printout of the map of Europe.

ACTIVITY NINE: Go to one of the web sites listed below, and research a play or concert you are interested in attending. E-mail this information to your instructor. Make sure you include the event name, date, location, ticket price, and any other information you believe is pertinent.

www.ticketmaster.com   www.sfsymphony.org

www.nytheatre.com   www.theatreticket.com

www.dallassummermusicals.com

www.myprimetime.com/play/culture

ACTIVITY TEN: Go to www.learn2.com and select **Tutorials**. Conduct a search to find step-by-step instructions on how to **Search the Internet Effectively**. Fill in the five steps below:

1. _____

2. _____

3. _____

4. _____

5. _____

Key the steps; then submit them to your instructor along with the printout of the steps from the web site.

Resource Guide

This Resource Guide provides examples of documents and forms prepared by the staff at the River Oaks Center office. Refer to these examples as directed in the instructions to your job assignments.

Most of the documents and forms will be familiar to you; others, however, may be unfamiliar. Be sure to use the format and style shown in the examples as you complete your work.

Example 1: Proofreaders' Marks

Keyed or printed copy may be corrected using special symbols called *Proofreaders' Marks* that indicate needed changes in the document.

The most commonly used proofreaders' marks are shown below:

SS	Single-space	bf or ~~	Boldface text
DS	Double-space	] [	Center copy
QS	Quadruple-space	]	Move right
≡	Capitalize	[	Move left
⁀	Close up	lc or /	Set in lowercase
ℓ	Delete	¶	Paragraph
∧	Insert	no ¶	No new paragraph
∧,	Insert comma	∽ tr	Transpose
⊙	Insert period	——	Underline
/#	Insert space	stet	Ignore correction
ℓ#	Delete space	◯ sp	Spell out

Procedures for Proofreading/Editing Documents:

1. After keying a document, use Spell Check to find and correct misspelled words.
2. Proofread the document word for word to find errors not detected by the Spell Check. Such corrections include spelling of proper names, incorrect word usage, grammatical or punctuation errors, and additions or omissions in the text.
3. Correct any errors detected and save the document.
4. Print the document, and use proofreaders' marks to mark any remaining errors for correction.
5. Correct the document again, if necessary. (Edit, save, and print the document.)

EXAMPLE 2: NEWS RELEASE

2" TM

News Release   **For Release:** Upon Receipt
                                                Contact: Elizabeth L. Clark

QS

0.5" → DALLAS, TX, June 3, 20—. Rutherford, Inc., of Dallas is proud to announce the

opening of a premier children's shoe store, Wonderful World of Shoes, at River Oaks Centre.

The exciting 12,000-square-foot store will be located between Starlight Jewelry and Conway

Cosmetics and is adjacent to Bachmont's.

Wonderful World of Shoes is a new concept in Dallas, and the store will feature a

complete selection of quality children's shoes in a fun atmosphere. "The store will have an

1" LM → authentic Western atmosphere—from the Austin stone storefront to the mesquite and pecan   1" RM ←

wood fixtures inside," says owner Edwina Smithen. "We want the store to have a true Texas

Hill Country feeling that is fun for children." Inside Wonderful World of Shoes, children will

enjoy sitting on a genuine leather horse saddle, watching videos on a giant screen, or riding atop

a moving mechanical horse.

Customers will appreciate the collection of top-quality children's footwear that

Wonderful World of Shoes provides. Look for a selection unparalleled in Dallas, including

brands such as Baby Doll, Adventure Kids, Wonderoos, Brooks, and more.

The new store will have its Grand Opening on July 8, 20—, at 10 a.m. with live ponies, a

balloon artist, and free giveaways. Customers may bring their Super Value Club cards to receive

discount coupons. These coupons will be provided by radio station KBIX.

News Release

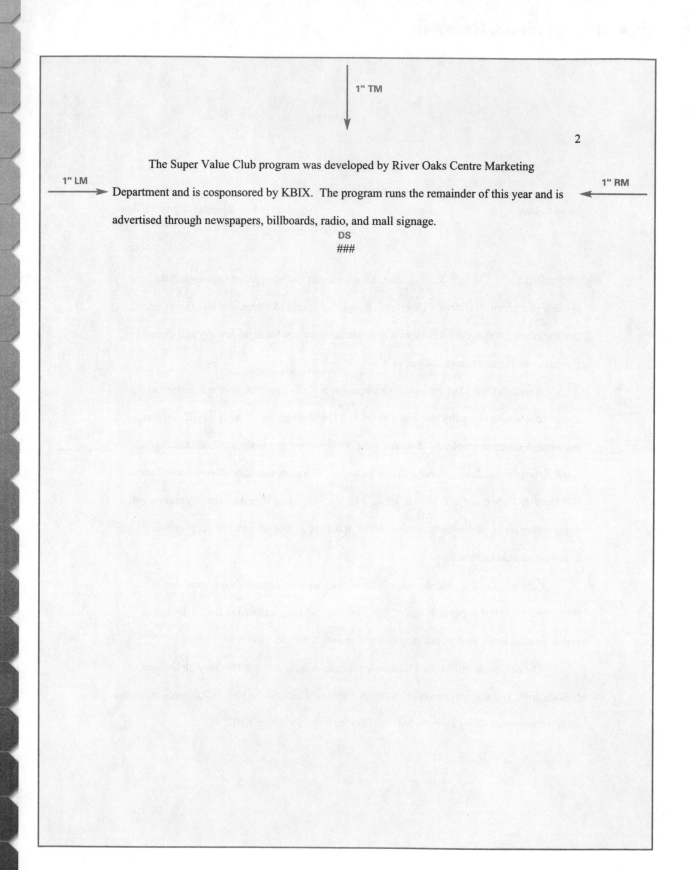

1" TM

2

The Super Value Club program was developed by River Oaks Centre Marketing

1" LM

Department and is cosponsored by KBIX. The program runs the remainder of this year and is

1" RM

advertised through newspapers, billboards, radio, and mall signage.

DS

###

News Release

EXAMPLE 3: PERSONAL BUSINESS LETTER

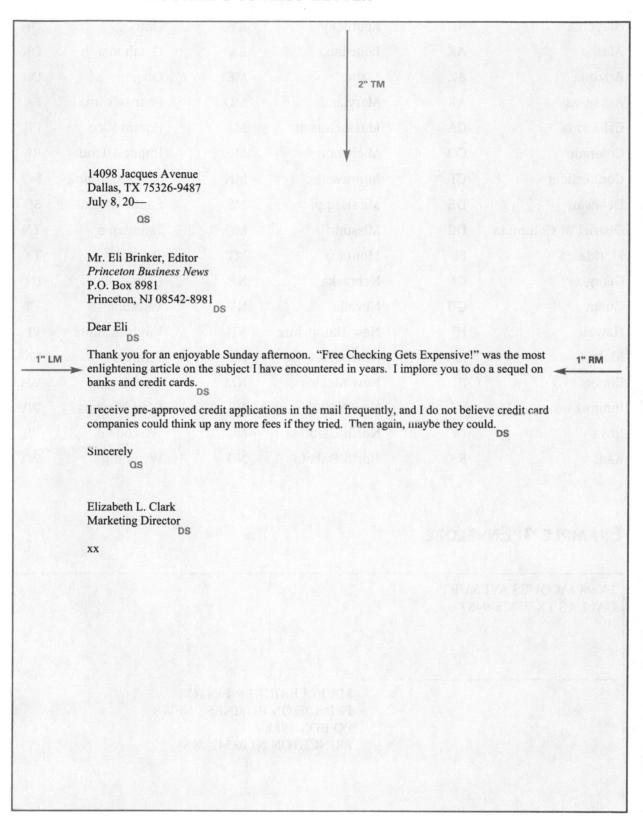

2" TM

14098 Jacques Avenue
Dallas, TX 75326-9487
July 8, 20—

QS

Mr. Eli Brinker, Editor
Princeton Business News
P.O. Box 8981
Princeton, NJ 08542-8981

DS

Dear Eli

DS

1" LM → Thank you for an enjoyable Sunday afternoon. "Free Checking Gets Expensive!" was the most ← 1" RM
enlightening article on the subject I have encountered in years. I implore you to do a sequel on
banks and credit cards.

DS

I receive pre-approved credit applications in the mail frequently, and I do not believe credit card
companies could think up any more fees if they tried. Then again, maybe they could.

DS

Sincerely

QS

Elizabeth L. Clark
Marketing Director

DS

xx

STATE ABBREVIATIONS

Alabama	AL	Kentucky	KY	Ohio	OH
Alaska	AK	Louisiana	LA	Oklahoma	OK
Arizona	AZ	Maine	ME	Oregon	OR
Arkansas	AR	Maryland	MD	Pennsylvania	PA
California	CA	Massachusetts	MA	Puerto Rico	PR
Colorado	CO	Michigan	MI	Rhode Island	RI
Connecticut	CT	Minnesota	MN	South Carolina	SC
Delaware	DE	Mississippi	MS	South Dakota	SD
District of Columbia	DC	Missouri	MO	Tennessee	TN
Florida	FL	Montana	MT	Texas	TX
Georgia	GA	Nebraska	NE	Utah	UT
Guam	GU	Nevada	NV	Vermont	VT
Hawaii	HI	New Hampshire	NH	Virgin Islands	VI
Idaho	ID	New Jersey	NJ	Virginia	VA
Illinois	IL	New Mexico	NM	Washington	WA
Indiana	IN	New York	NY	West Virginia	WV
Iowa	IA	North Carolina	NC	Wisconsin	WI
Kansas	KS	North Dakota	ND	Wyoming	WY

EXAMPLE 4: ENVELOPE

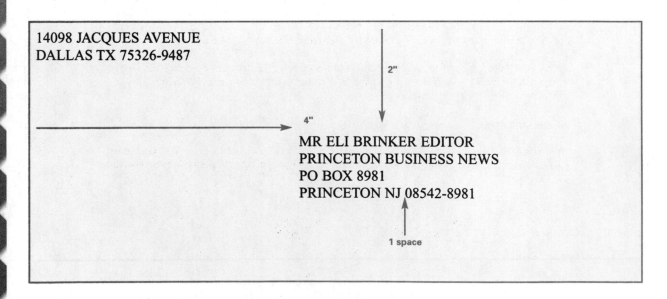

14098 JACQUES AVENUE
DALLAS TX 75326-9487

2"

4"

MR ELI BRINKER EDITOR
PRINCETON BUSINESS NEWS
PO BOX 8981
PRINCETON NJ 08542-8981

1 space

ENVELOPE

EXAMPLE 5: TWO-PAGE INTEROFFICE MEMO

2" TM

TO: Tab   Distribution
        DS
FROM: Tab   Ms. Tawana C. Stiles
                DS
DATE: Tab   June 18, 20—
                DS
SUBJECT:Tab MEDIA DINNER FOR COUNTRY JAMBOREE
                DS

As a kickoff for Country Jamboree, we have invited selected media to a "Chuck Wagon" dinner from 6:30 p.m. to approximately 8 p.m. on Friday, July 30, in the Showcase Theater.
        DS

Between 100 and 150 people will be attending this dinner. We need the following assistance from various departments.
        DS

Food Service
        DS

1" LM

Personnel from Tophand Management will be bringing in a chef early Friday morning to cook ribs. We will give you a definite attendance number on Wednesday so the correct number of ribs can be thawed and delivered on Friday morning.
        DS

1" RM

In addition, we will need baked beans, cole slaw, corn on the cob, iced tea, and soft drinks for this group as well as condiments, plates, dinnerware, and so on.
        DS

A number of food service personnel dressed in appropriate Western wear will be needed.
        DS

Security
        DS

We would like all guests to enter the park through the main entrance. They will be instructed to ask for directions at the ticket office. When they do, personnel should provide them with the directions sheet and instruct them to park as near as possible to the back gate. They can then walk to the Showcase Theater area. Guests should arrive between 6 p.m. and 7 p.m.
        DS

Personnel from Tophand Management and entertainers who will be working during the dinner should enter through the personnel gate and be directed to park on the road behind the arcade. (This will involve 20-25 people.)
        DS

Show Operations
        DS

We would like the Silver Canyon Band to perform from 6:30 p.m. until 8 p.m. The band must set up its sound system at the Showcase Theater by 5:45 p.m. and begin performing no later than 6:30.

Ms. Tawana C. Stiles
Page 2
June 18, 20—
DS

1" TM

1" LM   1" RM

The band will perform a variety of Top 40 hits. There will be a small dance floor for those who would like to dance to the music.
DS

We will use the band's microphones and speaker system to make our announcements. There will be no need to set up our system.
DS

xx

Two-Page Interoffice Memo

EXAMPLE 6: ANNOUNCEMENT

Center vertically and horizontally on page

RIVER OAKS CENTRE MERCHANTS ASSOCIATION

WILL HOLD ITS MONTHLY MEETING

FROM 8:30–9:30 A.M.

ON WEDNESDAY, AUGUST 5.

PLEASE MAKE EVERY EFFORT

TO ATTEND THIS IMPORTANT MEETING.

EXAMPLE 7: FOUR-COLUMN TABLE WITH HEADINGS

Center vertically and horizontally on page

CANDY FOR EASTER EGG HUNT			
Item	**Description**	**Number of Pieces**	**Price**
2423	Chocolate Covered Eggs	100	$8.26
1390	Taffy Easter Eggs	100	$6.89
3550	Caramel-Filled Eggs	125	$9.58
2050	Assorted Miniatures	200	$10.85
5835	Bubble Gum Bunnies	200	$8.59

Four-Column Table with Headings

EXAMPLE 8: MLA REPORT

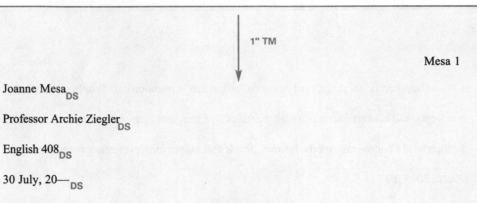

1" TM

Mesa 1

Joanne Mesa_{DS}

Professor Archie Ziegler_{DS}

English 408_{DS}

30 July, 20—_{DS}

E-Mail Shopping_{DS}

0.5" → Coming soon to home computer screens everywhere is the largest mall in the known universe. It will be open 24 hours a day, seven days a week. The only things a person will need to access this mall are an Internet connection and a credit card. Imagine no crowds at the cash register and no jam-packed parking lots. This is called "cybershopping."

<u>Cybershopping</u>

1" LM → Cybershopping has one small hitch: security. Protecting data privacy and verifying buyer and seller identities are major concerns in the virtual shopping mall. However, several companies, eager to become consumers' passports to cybershopping, are offering software and safety procedures to help solve security problems. ← 1" RM

If experts are right, Americans may soon be cybershopping for everything from wrenches to roses. Currently, about 400 electric malls have addresses on the Net. Comet Communications, a New York market research firm, predicts that sales through these systems will escalate from the current $75 million to $6 billion in the next five years. (Miller, 1998, 82)

<u>Internet</u>

The lure is convenience, but convenience may come at a price beyond on-line charges. Most transactions on the Internet involve credit cards and e-mail messages sent electronically between consumers and merchants. E-mail and credit cards can be a risky combination.

1" TM

Mesa 2

The potential for credit card scams on the Internet is phenomenal. People set up phony

storefronts, and hackers intercept e-mail messages with purchase-order information. Also, with

the high level of anonymity on the Internet, people feel safe in misrepresenting themselves.

(Haust, 2000, 10-11)

<u>Browser Software</u>

An Internet customer, using any browser software, keys <u>www.internetmci.com</u> to access

the Internet's home page. He or she uses the mouse to get to a screen describing the services and

stores in the Internet. The customer scans the mall "aisles"—lists arranged by item or store—

and clicks on the store to be browsed, displaying the store's home page, which has graphics and

text describing its wares. Each merchant designs his or her own storefront using guidelines

established by the software. The customer clicks on an item listed on the store's home page. An

order form pops up on which he or she specifies the size, color, and quantity of the item

selected, as well as any other pertinent information. A payment-server software is then used to

place the order. To do more shopping, the customer clicks on an icon to place the ordered items

1" TM

Mesa 3

Works Cited

Haust, Julia, Andrew Wall, and Shara Heisler. "Attention, E-Mail Shoppers." <u>Bloomberg</u>

0.5" → <u>Personal Business</u>. May 2000: 10-11.

Miller, James, Michele Goldring, and Bernie Weber. "Payment Server Software." <u>Cyberlines</u>.

December 1998: 82.

Wong, Michael. "Electronic Marketplace." <u>Internet Shopping News</u>. February 1999: 36-37.

All DS

EXAMPLE 9: BLOCK LETTER

2701 Rochelle Drive
Dallas, TX 75260-4244
Phone (972)555-0101
FAX (972)555-0179
www.riveroakscentre.com

2" TM

July 28, 20—ₒ QS

Miss Terri Durcham, President
Transworld Advertising
204 Parnell Street, Suite A
Chicago, IL 60636-3412 DS

Dear Miss Durcham: DS

VOLUNTEERS FOR SUMMER PROMOTION DS

Speaking with you on Thursday was a pleasure. This letter serves as a follow-up to our conversation regarding your assistance in securing a group of volunteers to assist with River Oaks Centre's Summer Promotion DS

1" LM

1" RM

As discussed, you will contact the PTA organizations to solicit their assistance for this project. In return, they will each receive a $500 donation. We will hold an informational meeting prior to the onset of the promotion to brief the volunteers DS

The attached schedule outlines the dates, times, number of volunteers, and hours needed to fulfill the project's objectives. I look forward to working with you DS

Sincerely, QS

Elizabeth L. Clark
Marketing Director DS

xx DS

Enclosure DS

c Roger Shea Pressley

Block Letter

◆

EXAMPLE 10: SIX-COLUMN TABLE WITH HEADINGS AND SHADING

Center vertically and horizontally on page

CLIMATE IN DALLAS					
Month	Average Rainfall in Inches	Average High Temperature (Fahrenheit)	Average Low Temperature (Fahrenheit)	Average Time of Sunrise	Average Time of Sunset
January	1.31	56°	35°	7:33	5:59
February	1.97	59°	38°	7:17	6:24
March	2.34	68°	46°	6:45	6:46
April	3.88	75°	55°	6:40	7:50
May	4.63	83°	63°	6:38	8:27
June	2.94	91°	71°	6:35	8:41
July	2.23	95°	74°	6:45	8:39
August	2.23	95°	74°	7:04	8:15
September	2.94	88°	67°	7:13	7:42
October	3.00	79°	57°	7:18	6:35
November	2.20	67°	46°	7:20	5:41
December	1.92	58°	37°	7:24	5:39

EXAMPLE 11: MINUTES

2" TM

SUMMARY MINUTES RIVER OAKS CENTRE MERCHANTS ASSOCIATION MEETING _{DS}

July 18, 20— _{QS}

The regular monthly meeting of the ROC Merchants Association was held on Tuesday, July 18, 20—, in the Vista Room of the Centre. President Todd McCain called the meeting to order at 1 p.m. _{DS}

Committee members in attendance: Elizabeth L. Clark, Marketing Director of River Oaks Centre; Lou Daily, Manager of Manford, Inc.; Connor Rehm, Manager of Toys Delux; Bella Arroyo-Wright, Manager of Beauty Spot; Bruce McHenry, Manager of Zip's Ice Cream; Lucinda Estrada, Manager of First-Choice Foods; Zelda Smithe, Manager of Barbosa Clothiers; and George Owens, Manager of George's Coats. _{DS}

1" LM

1" RM

Recorder of minutes: Zelda Smithe. _{DS}

1. The minutes of the June 21, 20—, meeting were read and approved. _{DS}

2. President Todd McCain called the meeting to order at 8:35 a.m. and welcomed all to the meeting.

3. The school cash program has just been completed. Results will be reported at the August staff meeting. Customer response has been extremely positive, and participation in the program has remained steady.

4. The Fall Home Show presented by Premier Promotions will be held September 8-14 throughout the Centre.

5. The Better Business Showcase sponsored by the Chamber of Commerce will be held throughout the Centre September 18-22, 20—.

6. The June financials were distributed. Lucinda Estrada requested a motion to accept the treasurer's report. The motion was accepted by Bruce McHenry and seconded by Connor Rehm.

7. McCain asked if there was any new business. He called for a motion to adjourn. Estrada so moved, and Rehm seconded the motion. The meeting was adjourned at 9:45 a.m.

Minutes

EXAMPLE 12: UNBOUND REPORT WITH TEXTUAL CITATIONS AND REFERENCES

2" TM

PROGRAMS AND ACTIVITIES REPORT

QS

0.5"

The following report outlines the major programs and activities accomplished at

River Oaks Centre for the second quarter.

DS

<u>Buck-for-Buck Auction</u>

DS

The Buck-for-Buck Auction was held Sunday in Folger's Court. More than 900

registered Buck-for-Buck customers participated in this event. A professional auctioneer

auctioned off the prizes. The winner of the car was a prize sponsor. The winner of the boat

made more than $12,000 in returns after the auction and, therefore, was not awarded the boat.

1" LM

1" RM

Local counsel is handling this case.

DS

<u>Super Value Club</u>

DS

Super Value Club membership grew to 5,700 members by the end of the month. All

existing members received a Super Value Club card introducing this new program. These

customers were invited to validate their cards and to receive their monthly discounts at the River

Oaks Centre Information Booth.

DS

<u>Frequent Buyer Program</u>

DS

The employee frequent buyer program continues to be a success. To date, more than 300

employees have entered the monthly drawings for prizes such as a microwave oven, mall gift

certificates, and U.S. Savings Bonds.

Unbound Report with Textual Citations and References

2

Good Values Campaign _{DS}

      Continuation of the Good Values campaign was used to advertise the sidewalk sale and

other promotional events. Advertising of the Super Value Club was achieved through direct

mail, through newspapers, and on radio station KCAR. Super Value Club newspaper advertising

appeared in *The Dallas News* and *The Plano Star*. _{DS}

Arts & Crafts Show _{DS}

      The Arts & Crafts Show was held and generated $7,000 in additional revenues for the

Merchants Association. The Handmade in America Show produced the show.

      Advertisements were placed in *Tourist Host, See Magazine,* and *Visitor's Guide.*

Additional advertising appeared in the Chamber of Commerce Visitors Guide and on the Dallas

area map. Both documents are distributed to visitors who visit the area and are mailed to people

who call the Chamber requesting information about the area.

3

REFERENCES _{QS}

Dallas Official Tourists' Guide. Publication of The Dallas Convention and Visitors Bureau.
    1999-2000 ed., Dallas, Texas. _{DS}

River Oaks Monthly. Publication of River Oaks Centre, Summer 2000 ed., Dallas, Texas.

Unbound Report with Textual Citations and References

EXAMPLE 13: CALENDAR OF EVENTS

1" TM

VACATION SWEEPSTAKES
QS

1.   <u>Contest Deadline</u>—July 15: To enter the Last-Chance Vacation Prize Drawing, complete an Official Entry Form, available at River Oaks Centre. Drop it into the official "Register To Win" entry box located at either the KACR remote or the Customer Service Center at River Oaks Centre. DS

2.   <u>Prize Drawing</u>—August 1: The drawing to award the vacation prizes will be conducted on August 1 by River Oaks Centre management. Winners will be selected at random from among all eligible entries received. DS

3.   <u>Validations</u>—August 5: Entrants agree to be bound by these rules and all decisions of River Oaks Centre, whose decisions are final on all aspects of the sweepstakes. Each potential winner will be notified by electronic mail and/or overnight delivery and may be required to sign and return within 14 days of delivery an Affidavit of Compliance with these official rules, a Prize Release, and a Publicity Release for use of his/her name and likeness without further compensation. Failure to sign and return these forms within such time period may result in forfeiture of prize. No responsibility is assumed for Internet and telecommunication interruptions or problems of lost, late, or stolen mail. Sweepstakes entries and other materials are void if they are incomplete or not legible or if they contain errors. DS

1" LM
with 0.5"
hanging
indent →

1" RM

4.   <u>Participation</u>—July 15: Sweepstakes are open only to legal residents 16 years of age or older of the state of Texas. Employees and their immediate families of General Growth, River Oaks Centre, KACR, and River Oaks Centre merchants and their respective parent companies, vendors, subsidiaries, affiliates, and agencies are not eligible to win any prize. By entering, you agree to release, discharge, and hold harmless General Growth, River Oaks Centre, KACR, and River Oaks Centre merchants from all claims or damages arising out of participation in this sweepstakes and/or acceptance of any prize. This sweepstakes is subject to all federal, state, and local laws and regulations. DS

5.   <u>Prizes</u>—August 1: Grand prize is a five-day cruise package for two from Galveston, Texas, aboard the "Fun Ship" *Celebration*. The grand prize includes meals, entertainment, and lodging for two people. An ocean-view cabin is provided. Transportation to and from Galveston is not included. Gratuities and personal purchases are not included. Travel dates are subject to available/advance reservations. Restrictions and blackout dates may apply. Winner and travel companion are responsible for any necessary passports and expenses not listed above and must sign a travel release prior to awarding of prize. Second-place prize is a three-night trip for two to Cancun, Mexico. This prize is provided by KACR radio station. The trip includes round-trip, nonstop

1" TM

2

airfare from DFW Airport to Cancun, Mexico, and accommodations for three nights at the Kalina Beach Hotel in Cancun. Trip does not include airport/hotel transfers or departure taxes or fuel surcharges.

6. <u>General Prize Terms</u>—August 15: All prizes must be claimed and redeemed by August 15. There is a limit of one Vacation Prize per household. There will be no substitution or transfer of prizes except with the sponsor's permission or where required by law. If prizes become unavailable, sponsor may substitute a prize of equal or greater value. All federal, state, and local taxes and fees for receipt of prize are the sole responsibility of the winner. If any prizewinner is a minor, the prize will be awarded to the parent or legal guardian. Odds of winning depend on the number of eligible entries received.

7. <u>List of Prizewinners</u>—September 1: A list of prizewinners will be available to those who send a stamped, self-addressed envelope to River Oaks Centre, 2701 Rochelle Drive, Dallas, TX 75260-4244.

EXAMPLE 14: MODIFIED BLOCK LETTER

River Oaks Centre

2701 Rochelle Drive
Dallas, TX 75260-4244
Phone (972)555-0101
FAX (972)555-0179
www.riveroakscentre.com

2" TM

August 3, 20—
QS

Mrs. Kristen Stewart, Manager
Starlight Jewelry
2701 Rochelle Drive, Suite 1103
Dallas TX 75260-4244
DS

Dear Mrs. Stewart:
DS

SCHEDULE OF EVENTS
DS

1" LM

1" RM

Enclosed is the latest schedule of events. As you can see, we look forward to an extremely busy and prosperous spring!
DS

Please distribute this information to the appropriate personnel in your store. Also, you need to begin printing the name *River Oaks Centre* along with your store name and date on all your receipts. We need this information on receipts for the school cash promotion.
DS

If you have any questions, please do not hesitate to contact us.
DS

Sincerely,
QS

Elizabeth L. Clark
Marketing Director
DS

xx
DS

Enclosure
DS

c Desiree Suppan

Modified Block Letter

EXAMPLE 15: TWO-PAGE BLOCK LETTER

Wild Water Fun Park
1000 Regents Boulevard
Atlanta, GA 31139-1974
770-555-0160   fax: 770-555-0170
www.wildwaterfun.com

2" TM

March 30, 20—
QS

Mr. Pedro Blanco
2538 Chevy Drive
Atlanta, GA 30331-2033
DS

Dear Mr. Blanco
DS

WILD WATER FUN PASS
DS

Last summer was an exciting time for the management staff of Wild Water Fun Park. Part of the excitement was in meeting you and serving you as our guest. We trust that you enjoyed Wild Water and that you felt your visit represented a good summertime entertainment value.
DS

1" LM

Summer will be here again before long, and we would like to help you get ready for it by making season passes available now. Buying a season pass by June 30 will save you $15 on an individual pass and $40 on a family pass. Of course, a pass would be a great gift!
DS

1" RM

There are several other reasons to buy a season pass this year, including:
DS

0.5"

1. A chance to win a trip for four to Walt Disney World and Epcot.
DS

2. An opportunity to see the spectacular water attraction that will be introduced this year. Watch closely for more details!

3. Free parking and unlimited free admission. (Season passes are nontransferable.)

4. Three dollars off each of five $18.95 general admission tickets to Wild Water. Use these tickets for your friends or family.

5. Twenty percent off all regularly priced Atlanta Braves souvenir items at the Swim Shop. (Offer is good this year only.)

6. Twenty-five percent off all Wild Water Gift Shop logo items and twenty percent off all other regularly priced items. (Offer is good this year only.)

1" TM

Mr. Pedro Blanco
Page 2
March 30, 20—
DS

7. Ten percent off all purchases at Park Pizza, located on Hamilton Avenue near Waycross Drive. (Offer applies July 30 through August 31.)

8. Five dollars off an adult admission and $1 off a child's admission to Stone Mountain. (Offer applies July 31 to September 30 with a one-coupon limit per season for each pass holder.)

We hope to hear from you soon about buying a pass and entering the trip contest to Walt Disney World and Epcot. Call 770-555-0160 to order your season pass, or visit the Park Office Monday through Friday between 9 a.m. and 5 p.m.

Again, we enjoyed having you as a guest during the past summer and look forward to your patronage.

Sincerely

Jack C. Garner
Vice President of Show Productions

xx

Two-Page Block Letter

EXAMPLE 16: AGENDA

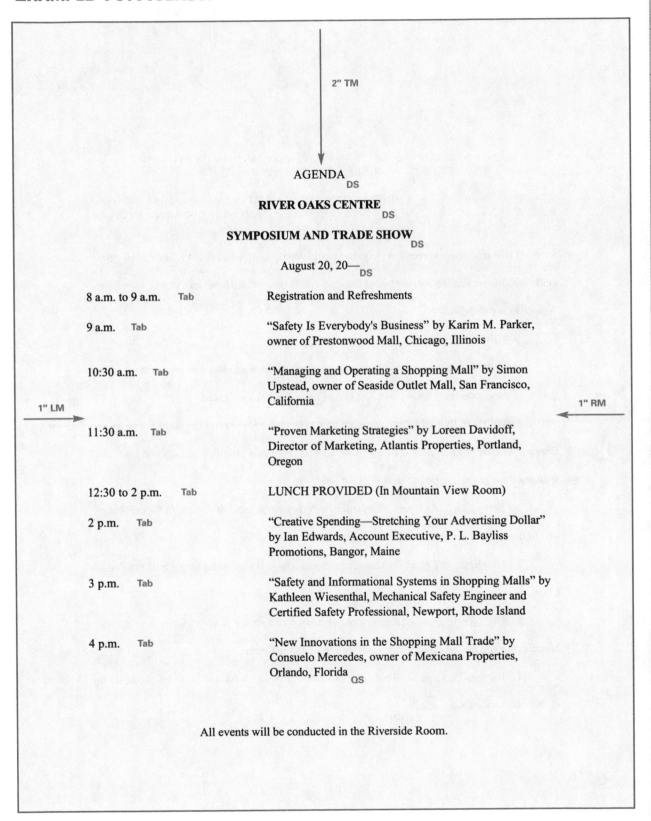

2" TM

AGENDA
DS

RIVER OAKS CENTRE
DS

SYMPOSIUM AND TRADE SHOW
DS

August 20, 20—
DS

8 a.m. to 9 a.m.	Tab	Registration and Refreshments
9 a.m.	Tab	"Safety Is Everybody's Business" by Karim M. Parker, owner of Prestonwood Mall, Chicago, Illinois
10:30 a.m.	Tab	"Managing and Operating a Shopping Mall" by Simon Upstead, owner of Seaside Outlet Mall, San Francisco, California
11:30 a.m.	Tab	"Proven Marketing Strategies" by Loreen Davidoff, Director of Marketing, Atlantis Properties, Portland, Oregon
12:30 to 2 p.m.	Tab	LUNCH PROVIDED (In Mountain View Room)
2 p.m.	Tab	"Creative Spending—Stretching Your Advertising Dollar" by Ian Edwards, Account Executive, P. L. Bayliss Promotions, Bangor, Maine
3 p.m.	Tab	"Safety and Informational Systems in Shopping Malls" by Kathleen Wiesenthal, Mechanical Safety Engineer and Certified Safety Professional, Newport, Rhode Island
4 p.m.	Tab	"New Innovations in the Shopping Mall Trade" by Consuelo Mercedes, owner of Mexicana Properties, Orlando, Florida QS

1" LM

1" RM

All events will be conducted in the Riverside Room.

Agenda

EXAMPLE 17: LEGAL AGREEMENT

2" TM

RIVER OAKS CENTRE
DS

INDEMNITY AGREEMENT
QS

0.5" → THIS indemnity agreement ("Agreement") is made as of the 15th day of July, 20—, by

Gail Normington and the Storytellers of Brevard for the benefit of River Oaks Centre Merchants

Association ("ROCMA");

WITNESSETH;

WHEREAS, ROCMA is the landlord under various lease and license agreements for space

in the building commonly known as River Oaks Centre, Dallas, Texas; and

1" LM →   ← 1" RM

WHEREAS, ROCMA has contracted with "Gail Normington and the Storytellers of

Brevard" to have the Storytellers of Brevard Dickens' Carolers perform in the common area,

strolling through the Centre per the following schedule:

1. <u>Storytellers</u>. At 1 p.m., Storytellers will perform in front of Annona's for the group

of children who will congregate on the risers.

2. <u>Carolers</u>. At 2 p.m., the Carolers will perform on the platform set up near the Food

Court.

3. <u>Gail Normington</u>. At 3 p.m., a performance will be given in the common area as Gail

Normington and her group of performers stroll through the Centre.

4. <u>Brevard Dancers</u>. At 4 p.m., the dancers will present a routine on the platform set up

in front of Annona's.

1" TM

IN WITNESS WHEREOF, the parties hereto have hereunto set their hands and seals to

the Agreement the day and year first above written at Dallas County, Texas:

Signed, Sealed, and Delivered RIVER OAKS CENTRE MERCHANTS
in the Presence of ASSOCIATION, INC.
 DS

0.5" ——▶ (Corporate Seal)
 QS

_____ _____
 DS
0.5" ——▶ ("Promoter") 0.5" from ——▶ ("Association")
 center

EXAMPLE 18: THREE-COLUMN NEWSLETTER

Inside The Centre

August Special Events Update

A meeting of the River Oaks Centre Merchants Association will be held on August 11 at 9 a.m. concerning the Mall Money Promotion.

During the week of August 10, the Centre will feature a display of Z-cars. Radio station KACR will provide publicity.

The "Bear-able" Magic Show will begin on Saturday. We will have 25-30 executives from Corona Cola in the Centre to promote their product.

Fashion Show

Please mark your calendars for our fashion show, "Jump into Fall," on Saturday, September 3 at 3 p.m. The Trendsetters, our River Oaks Centre Teen Fashion Board, will be modeling the latest in back-to-school fashions from our stores.

If you would like to participate in our upcoming fashion show, please contact the Management Office.

Advertising Reminder

Our "Jump into Fall" fashion catalog will be direct mailed on September 3. The total distribution will be 100,000.

"Jump into Fall" black-and-white photography liner pages will break August 20 in *The Dallas News*.

Labor Day Sale black-and-white photography liner pages will break August 25 in *The Dallas News*.

We will be sending you a reminder on the remaining advertising events for this year. Please let us know if you have any questions or if we can be of help.

Cheerleading Association Cheer-Off

Area high school cheerleading squads will be vying the first Saturday in September for the chance to compete in the national cheerleading finals in Florida.

Judges from the local cheerleading association will be on hand to select the top cheerleading squad. Kid Braddick from the KCRE radio staff will be with us again to host this event.

Mall Management

Christian T. Brock,
General Manager

Elizabeth L. Clark,
Marketing Director

Hamilton Schrauff,
Leasing Manager

Christy Schall,
Operations Director

Scott K. Williams,
Chief of Security

SHOPPING